# RELEASING THE EMOTIONAL WOUND

"A thoughtful and elucidating book, Gina Goldfeder's *Releasing the Emotional Wound* will support anyone looking for deeper self-knowledge. Through a variety of psychological, emotional, and spiritual understandings and tools, Goldfeder guides readers to see their suffering clearly, move through it, and emerge with greater compassion and clarity. Her teaching that our wounds can become sources of deep wisdom and growth will help many people seeking to free themselves from the suffering they carry."

—**MARY MUELLER SHUTAN**, spiritual teacher and author of *Shadow Work for the Soul* and *The Spiritual Awakening Guide*

"*Releasing the Emotional Wound* offers a profound and illuminating journey into emotional healing. Through author Gina Goldfeder's empathy, experience, and authenticity, readers are guided to explore and understand their deepest emotional wounds—many rooted in childhood. Gina's book reads like a compassionate conversation that helps uncover pain while transforming it into growth. It explains the origins of emotional wounds, provides practical tools for healing, and invites readers to fully engage in life through reflective exercises. The result is a moving and transformative experience that leaves the reader with a renewed sense of calm and self-awareness."

—**MAYTE PRIDA**, TV, radio, and podcast host, motivational speaker, and author of *A Difficult Journey: My Battle with Cancer*

“What I treasure most in a healing book is the ability to offer more than one lens—to teach, to broaden, and to reveal new pathways of transformation. This book does precisely that. It offers a profound exploration of our emotional pain, its roots, and the diverse possibilities for healing and growth that arise from understanding it. A powerful companion for anyone seeking to mend childhood wounds beyond the limits of traditional psychology.”

—**YAEL EINI**, founder of Karmic Constellation, international teacher, and author of *Karma Healing*

“Gina Goldfeder offers a deeply compassionate and practical guide to understanding our most primal emotional wounds and the ways they quietly shape our lives. Her blend of clinical insight, rituals, and embodied practices creates a powerful pathway from old pain towards genuine inner transformation. This book gently shows that healing is not only possible but can become a profound opportunity to reclaim identity, connection, and joy. A wise, grounding, and beautifully written companion for anyone ready to move beyond their past and step into a more expansive way of being.”

—**MATHIAS KÜNLEN, M.D.,** neurologist, & **CHRISTINE WALDHAUSER-KÜNLEN**, journalist, authors of *Aura Surgery: Healing Karmic Patterns and Unconscious Conflicts in the Human Energy Field*

# RELEASING THE EMOTIONAL WOUND

## Shamanic and Psychological Tools to Transcend Trauma and Rebuild Your Life

Gina Goldfeder, Ph.D.

Translated by Gerardo Cárdenas

FINDHORN PRESS

Findhorn Press
One Park Street
Rochester, Vermont 05767
www.findhornpress.com

MIX
Paper | Supporting responsible forestry
FSC® C103098

Findhorn Press is a division of Inner Traditions International



Originally published in Spanish in 2023 by Ediciones Urano México as *Soltar La Herida*
English edition published in 2026 by Findhorn Press



---

**Disclaimer**

The information in this book is given in good faith and is neither intended to diagnose any physical or mental condition nor to serve as a substitute for informed medical advice or care. Please contact your health professional for medical advice and treatment. Neither author nor publisher can be held liable by any person for any loss or damage whatsoever which may arise from the use of this book or any of the information therein.

---

Cataloging-in-Publication data for this title is available from the Library of Congress

ISBN 979-8-88850-368-3 (print)
ISBN 979-8-88850-369-0 (ebook)

Printed and bound in the United States by Lake Book Manufacturing, LLC

10 9 8 7 6 5 4 3 2 1

Edited by Nicky Leach
Text design and layout by Richard Crookes
This book was typeset in Adobe Garamond Pro and Helvetica Neue

To send correspondence to the author of this book, mail a first-class letter to the author c/o Inner Traditions, One Park Street, Rochester, VT 05767, USA and we will forward the communication, or contact the author directly at **https://ginagoldfeder.com**.

I dedicate this book
—to my fellow travelers
— to the inner world
—to the survivors of a shipwreck
—to all those whose bodies have a story to tell
—to the person you have always been,
who exists outside of time,
ready to rediscover yourself
—and to my children, Marcos and Alexa,
my accomplices and the motivation
to release my wound.

# Contents

Part Two
I AM NOT THE WOUND –
TOOLS TO REMEMBER THIS

# Foreword

The book you hold in your hands is dazzling. I invoke the most symbolic meaning of this word "dazzle," because it makes a profound impact with the light it throws on its readers. Here, "to dazzle" means to discover, to pierce, to focus with great precision. Of course, it requires light, knowledge, and experience to stand alongside us.

We read it as if traveling through our own life, looking at it through the eyes of someone who knows the wounds, even the most secret ones; those that have remained in the shadows of our own consciousness. But this work does not settle at exposing them to the elements; it does not leave us stranded at that open door. With great care and empathy, it throws us a lifeline to heal and, in the process, find a new opportunity for life.

It almost seems like an act of magic, but it is the result of the career, research, and professionalism that its author puts in front of us, laying her cards on the table, guiding us through the emotional wounds that we all, in some way, carry through the years.

The first stop is to understand how these wounds originate: childhood and all its enormity, light, and shades, its inevitability and long resonance. It is impossible not to identify with each of the examples the author shares with us. By reading the stories of her patients, you read your own. You read your body; you read your story.

The prose is enriched with anecdotes, books, series, travels, and experiences. Someone very trustworthy whispers in your ear, as if telling you a story—the story of your own life; she is also telling you about her own life.

Gina Goldfeder, this always-smiling psychologist and writer, with her sharp and attentive eyes—right at "the prime of life," as Simone de Beauvoir would say, referring to the maturity of women—puts herself forward in each of the cases she narrates. We can feel the authenticity in every line because, her career notwithstanding, Gina is as human as her readers. She has been in the middle of the bull ring, sometimes fighting the bull and other times herself the bull, the sword, and the cape. That is where she has built the signs through which one can exit. The second part of the book is a toolbox for learning to live fully, a handy support for life.

The final part is about being in life, actively participating in it, though a series of exercises. For that, breathing is not enough; instead, we must set a date with ourselves and discover the wound as an opportunity for transformation.

As a writer and academic, I have accompanied many people in writing their works. I have never felt so "touched" by a support process as I was with this one. As the sessions with the author progressed during the first part, I had to stop at many of the invisible spaces where my own memories lay, face them, and recognize my own wound; with the tools and exercises of the second and third parts, I felt I could look it in the eye and then let it go.

There is something else—a sunny feeling as we put down the book, akin to the calm after the storm. It is like a smile landing on our body.

—**Ethel Krauze**, writer and TV presenter
Cuernavaca, Mexico, June 2023

# Preface

The writing of this book took place amid different symbolic and literal landscapes, from whence these words have emerged. It is a collection of voices: mine, everyone's. A portal opening paths to know the wound.

These are words that arise from the desert and its silence, which embraces everything. It is a place where the vastness of the horizon makes us imagine how far we might go to grab the opportunities life offers. The wound as a path.

These are words that have appeared from the trunks of sequoia trees and the foliage that gets lost in the sky, reminding us of our majestic yet diminutive existence.

These are words that have emerged from the trees embracing in a circle, sprouting from the whispers of people in the square and the sound of the bell tower of the parish, and watching time pass there, contemplating the past of our painful memories.

These are words that have manifested from silences, from looks, from secrets, from hidden places in convents and basements. Radiant words hidden in creative souls—words from the nooks where journals, books, canvases, and colors dwell.

These are words that come from loudspeakers, from prayers and mosques. Words from those I never met in person; words that flow from the laughter of my children, from the corridors of my childhood; words from shared landscapes, yours and mine; words from ancestral rituals, sketches and fragments of stories, speaking objects.

And thus, parallel, distant, concentric universes; shared wounds; memories of elusive memories and of mantras that cover the soul; and finally, arrival on solid ground with the clarity of our steps to reach its luminous landscapes.

# Introduction

The first time a patient enters my office, their motive is the same as everyone else's: to rid their life of the problem that makes them unhappy and to eradicate suffering as quickly as possible.

I listen attentively to every detail, how the wound was born, and the perspective the person has about their future. What a patient does not know is that their emotional wound is their opportunity—an opportunity that will enrich the experience of their transformation, the compass that will lead them back home.

As I write these lines, I realize that the idea may sound complicated, hard to believe, even impossible. But that is not the case. In over 30 years of working with patients—equivalent to almost 45,000 hours of therapy—I have concluded that the path to healing is always to stop fleeing from the wound, and instead, to know it, honor it, and transcend it.

This book aims to explain what the process of releasing the wound is like, in terms of turning it into an opportunity for life—to be reborn from what you thought you would never rise from.

"Someday you'll laugh at this."

"You'll find your strength through this pain."

"The best version of yourself is waiting for you in the near future."

These are phrases I say just a few sessions after starting the therapeutic process. Some people look at me in astonishment; others with disbelief, distrust, even anger. The reaction showing on their faces, more than in their words, shows me how arduous the path will be. Often, people do not believe it is possible to change and cling to their painful beliefs, which makes it difficult for them to take responsibility for their own lives.

There is a moment in our history when we are affected by the actions of others without having the ability to defend ourselves and set the necessary boundaries to care for our self-esteem. During childhood, this premise is feasible, since the child is vulnerable and dependent on the care of an adult; however, as a person grows, they acquire the ability to take responsibility for their own actions. Guilt and blame are variants of control.

> "If my life has been damaged, it is impossible for me to escape that destiny for a better one."

This is a collective thought that has worked from generation to generation. It is true that we have been hurt, even abandoned, and there are stories that can never be written, but when did we decide that this wound would define us forever? How long will we continue to pay homage to our victimizers, thus paralyzing our lives? When will we discover that we are free to change our story?

Releasing the emotional wound and creating a new identity is one of the most important challenges of being human, although not all of us know how to overcome the condition of victimhood and redefine who we really are. It seems that, over the years, our unresolved traumas become our interlocutors and allies, justifying the reasons that prevent us from living a full life, no matter how much we say we desire it.

We convince ourselves that we are the wound, the abandonment, and the lack of love, and this concept becomes ingrained in our cells. The power with which it settles in us makes us believe that the wound will never leave us, preventing us from being that version of ourselves that we have not yet met, and that scares us, the luminous being that we can become.

This book is divided into three parts. The first part describes the meaning of the emotional wound, its origin, and the process that follows when we identify so much with it that we are no longer able to see anything else in ourselves. The second part offers some tools to release the wound and strengthen the creation of a new personal identity. And the third part proposes exercises that affirm us in life using a new version of our personality.

The three parts together form the process of knowing, honoring, and releasing the wound and turning it into an opportunity for life. The tools and disciplines provided here are adaptations of therapeutic strategies I have created through a compilation of different psychological approaches and years of work in private practice.

It is important to clarify that terms for some key concepts in the book are used interchangeably in the text. This includes synonyms like "soul," "spirit," "inner world," "psychic dimension," even "symbolic content," and "unconscious," as well as various currents of thought and my own methodology, which adapts to the needs of each patient. I do not try to put my patients in boxes; rather, I develop a specific approach based on their needs, because anticipated diagnoses can be another reason for closed identification from which it is more difficult to emerge. In short, mine is an original approach whose effectiveness has been extensively tested in a wide group of people.

PART ONE

# IDENTIFYING WITH THE EMOTIONAL WOUND

# 1

# THE WOUND AS A PORTAL

I don't remember the day I stopped enjoying ruminating about the suffering from my past. My emotional wound had become my best friend, my confidant, from an early age. I had gotten used to the idea that the discomfort I lived with inside my home was a kind of destiny, perhaps because I could never escape it, so I just had to put on a brave face about it.

## Cooking over Low Heat

The wound is a dish cooked over low heat. In my case, I couldn't say exactly when it started, and I don't even remember my childhood well enough to draw any conclusions, but a few images and fragments occasionally visit my consciousness.

Some turn out to be others' stories filling gaps in my memories. This leads me to think that something unspeakable is blocking my memories of the past. I must confess that rather than feeling envious, I feel curiosity, admiration, and astonishment when it comes to those who remember their childhood in detail.

I could say that my wound began at birth with my mother's postpartum depression. It lasted my first year and a half of life, and she couldn't even hold me in her arms. I know this because it's what my father tells me, and because I see myself in a photograph where I am in front of my birthday cake with a number 2 candle, next to my grandmother and him.

Or perhaps it was the day when my mother helped a blind man cross the street and let go of my arm—or held it with greater force, I don't remember well—but what I do remember is that at that moment I felt immense anger, because it seemed to me that the man was more important to her than I was.

Or perhaps it was the day my father shouted at my mother in a restaurant and then we left alone and walked endless blocks home.

I also think that maybe it was when I was 15 and heard my father talking on the phone with his lover.

Or maybe it was three years later, when I heard my mother tell him that a "steady lover" no longer seemed right for her.

Or when my father cursed me in front of my mother's coffin.

## Stop Blaming the Past

I want to go back to the miracle of no longer enjoying blaming the past and identifying with my wound. Perhaps the exhaustion of being a victim for so many years left me immune, although saying this is unfair: I have worked throughout my life to stop being "my wound."

Perhaps it was the acceptance that there are events that have no solution and what remains is to look for an opportunity to live a worthy and meaningful existence.

As I said at the beginning, I don't remember how it happened, but I know two things for sure: After a long process of introspection and therapeutic support, one day I stopped being afraid and the pain turned into my strength. I say this with all the honesty I can muster.

A phrase from Bert Hellinger, creator of Family Constellations, comes to mind: "The wound, too, is part of life, and also the scar that indicates that the wound is healed, although the place remains vulnerable and warns us to proceed with care and caution."

But why do we identify with the emotional wound? Why does our identity cling to it?

Well, from my perspective, what we know most about ourselves is what hurts us— the ways we haven't been seen or the injuries we've received from those we love. When we connect with the pain, we learn what matters to us, what our values system is, and who we are in this world, especially when we are children.

The pain-wound that appears from who knows where—because I can almost guarantee that it always takes us by surprise—suddenly places us in a vulnerable place and we start to dwell there; some of us with insecurity, others with fear, anger, or desolation, and still others with self-doubt.

The wound is the opposite of love. You hurt me because you don't love me is the first thing a child thinks, or worse yet, perhaps the feeling of being unloved impregnates their skin making them believe that they "are that." Identification is one of the earliest processes of development, as we internalize everything we see on the outside as children, and that's how our personality is built.

Surprisingly, we hold onto our wound to find meaning in our story. One of the most significant themes I work on with couples in my private practice is validation of the inflicted wound; everything else flows, surfaces, and resolves if they can recognize the pain they have caused each other. It is a powerful formula that I invariably resort to and has yielded results for many years in my professional work.

## Signs

Imagine the wound as a portal that takes you to other dimensions, ranging from darkness to light. Visualize a subtle golden thread that connects those who have inflicted hurt with those who have been hurt. In that encounter, when there is an act of humility and then an honest attempt to repair the offense, the wound turns into love.

We don't let it go, because it gives us the opportunity to reclaim our individuality and to finally be seen. We don't let it go, because the ties that bind us to it can disappear, nor do we let it go as a matter of honor. However, when we regain what we have lost—whether someone has helped us repair it or we have repaired it ourselves—it is time to explore new horizons.

The wound is a solitary experience, a universe different from others, with its own language. There are various investigations and theories on this subject that explain the meaning, triggers, and different manifestations of an emotional wound. However, it has not yet been discovered how the brain chooses which experience will become traumatic and the meaning it carries.

Just as there are people who recognize the origin of their wound, there are others who deny it and bury it in forgetfulness in an attempt to have an apparently balanced life, thinking that the pain is already in the past, so it is better not to open the door for fear that the heart-wrenching childhood experience will drown them.

Despite the effort to keep the wound in exile, triggers will appear at a moment we least expect, connecting us with unresolved suffering.

These triggers can be as subtle or trivial as, for instance, seeing a scene in a movie that suddenly provokes uncontrollable tears; hearing a piece of music that brings back memories we had forgotten or blocked; a word or phrase written on a billboard confronting us; or more complex, noticeable, or transcendent triggers, such as the death of a family member, the birth of a child, a divorce, a job change, a move, an inheritance or financial loss, to mention a few.

Any of these events marks a life change, putting us to the test and connecting us with what we fear, what has hurt us, or what we have forgotten in order to survive. Then, the wound emerges as a call or reminder of what has not yet been resolved or alerts us to protect ourselves from situations that resemble that old injury.

Just yesterday, I was watching the animated movie Coco with my children, and the plot emotionally overwhelmed me: A 12-year-old boy is transported to the world of the dead, where he reconnects with his great-grandfather and the legacy of his music. The dead inhabit their own world but disintegrate and disappear forever when they cease to exist in the memory of the living. The message revolves around what "definitive death" represents, referring to the fact that the forgetfulness of the living toward the dead is, in reality, the last death of a human being.

"Why are you crying?" my son asked.

I couldn't explain that accumulated and unresolved grief had collapsed in my throat; that the tears flowing from my eyes embodied years of silence and impossibility surrounding the death of my parents. The theme of the movie had made me think of my mother, and how little I remember her since she passed away, and my father, whom I have also forgotten, in order to survive our painful story.

The repair occurs when we validate such experiences, recognize the impact they have had on our lives, are able to release them, and change their place in our world.

# 2

# ONCE UPON A TIME . . .

Some people can date exactly, right down to the time, when they suffered their emotional wound. Many more of us, though, don't know why we feel bewildered, anxious, depressed, or are having panic attacks at certain moments in our lives and times of day.

## The 6 p.m. Terror

On Thursdays, Alfonso suffered intense periods of anxiety around 6 p.m., always on the same day as his therapy session, when his wife went out with her friends.

After a long process of therapeutic investigation, we discovered that the day, time, and feeling of abandonment coincided with a particular Thursday during his childhood.

He had hidden under the couch at 6 p.m. and his mother hadn't bothered to look for him; in fact, no one in his family had noticed his absence. "It was as if I didn't exist. I could have disappeared, and no one would have cared," he said.

He recalled falling asleep under the couch and staying there all night unnoticed by any of his family.

## No Solid Ground to Set Foot on

Sonia suffered from multiple phobias, including agoraphobia (a type of anxiety disorder related to open spaces and being alone, among other fears), in addition to her fear of water, nights, and strangers. Together, we discovered that from a young age, she had been taught to distrust the outside world, because "strangers can abuse you," as her parents used to say.

Another powerful message was the loyalty required of each family member in downplaying any personal ambitions or achievements that could jeopardize family unity. "You will end up alone, and no one will love you," was an echo that resonated in her memory every time she tried to pursue a professional project or have a romantic relationship. In families where incest takes place, it is often the case that distrust of "outsiders" is used as a way of keeping the practice secret and maintaining control over the victims.

Sonia bought a car that she parked in her garage for over a year because she was too scared to drive it more than a block. Her insecurity in navigating the city alone led her to use public transportation, so her commute to my office took over two and a half hours. She also had a panic attack during her first swimming lesson, even though the instructor reassured her that she was standing on solid ground.

Sonia's wound stemmed from silently witnessing the sexual abuse of her older sisters by their father without being able to do anything about it.

## Rewriting Your Story

Once Upon a Time is a therapeutic exercise I assign my patients, in which I ask them to write a short story on a sheet of paper about their emotional wound and how they have become accustomed to it. When they finish, they must turn over the sheet of paper and rewrite the story without the wound and describe the experience of feeling free from that darkness. Afterwards, they read both stories aloud and then, together, we proceed to a minute of silence as a kind of posthumous tribute.

The therapeutic intention of this task is "dis-identification" from the wound; that is, the person can observe themselves as separate from the traumatic event that occurred to them. This opens up the possibility of a new internal narrative that allows them to occupy a different place within their life experience.

Every time I hear both sides of the same story, I am intrigued to know what the patient wants to do with that narrative. Do they want to use it as a calling card? Is it a family legacy they want to continue? A motivation for change? A good luck charm, or perhaps a sentence?

Within each narrative, there is a predominant element from which the patient chooses to tell the story. The choice of theme arises from the particular significance that the wound represents for them; thus, a story can revolve around rejection and the impact it has on their life, or abandonment, shame, disloyalty, or any other relevant emotional aspect that determines the course of events and the final outcome of the narration. When the person has the opportunity to share the story of their traumatic experience, in some way, they force themselves to reconstruct the representation they have of their wound and, by restructuring it on the other side of the page, the brain's functioning and the way of perceiving and feeling that circumstance are modified.

A Year Ago is another effective therapeutic exercise, in which I ask the patient to simulate a conversation with me discussing events, changes, transformations, and achievements that have not yet happened to them, but we mention them as if they had already occurred.

For example: "Do you remember a year ago, when setting boundaries was hard for you?"

Here, I ask them to use the voice of their future self who has already overcome the challenges and is clear about the path traveled. After a few minutes of maintaining this narrative, the energy begins to rise to create an atmosphere in which we both believe that what we have said is true; that is, we have opened a window to possibility.

Another strategy I use is to add the phrase "until now" to emphasize the change in attitude the patient has achieved based on their painful and limiting experiences. Within this active imagination of the future, this phrase marks the end of the difficulty: "I did not know how to set boundaries . . . until now."

## Life Coach

Miriam wrote a story of her life related to her mother's abandonment. In describing that wound, she felt lonely and faced extreme situations during her youth, from struggling to make ends meet to the experience of suffering abuse from her boss at work. The emotional abandonment by her mother made it impossible for her to seek help, so she kept secret the various forms of violence she experienced.

During her marriage and motherhood, the shadow of her mother's abandonment reemerged, causing depression and anxiety attacks that made it difficult for her to relate to her children and husband. On the back of the page, in the story without the wound, she described a life in which she was self-assured, capable of pursuing her professional and personal goals without fear of poverty or abuse. The interesting discovery in this case was uncovering, alongside Miriam, aspects she had not imagined, such as her assertiveness in seeking opportunities to start her own business and become a personal image coach, two dreams she had considered impossible in the past.

## Nostalgia for the Lost Home

The place from which a person identifies with their emotional wound is the lane along which their life will progress. By place, I mean the thoughts and emotions accompanying that wound, arising from the social, educational, cultural, and religious context of the person.

Let's take rejection as an example.

Natalia is of European origin and hails from a culture where free expression, teamwork, professionalism, planning, and organization are fundamental values within her accustomed work environment. Her motivation for therapy was her frustration at not feeling part of her work group. Over a year and a half of therapeutic work, we addressed the collective rejection she received each time she proposed a project. The difference between the European and Mexican cultures turned out to be her biggest obstacle to performing successfully, eventually leading her to resign.

As therapy progressed, we discovered that her childhood wound was rejection from her mother, and her work experience had triggered that past pain. Her childhood wound revolved around a memory of when she was seven years old:

> "My mother locked herself in her room for a year, lying down with the lights turned off. During that time, she didn't look at me, and my father was in charge of feeding her and taking me to school. In the afternoons, I was left alone while he went to work. Family meals and tea gatherings to talk about things that excited us and made us happy as a family stopped happening. My mother tried to take her own life a couple of times, which made me question if I was not important for her to decide to stay with me in this world."

When Natalia experienced disapproval at work, this rejection became a reminder of her childhood wound, the result of living with a depressed mother who stopped looking at her and providing the care and protection she needed. When she connected with her pain, homesickness for the country of her birth emerged, including everything she had left behind when she moved countries, such as her language, nature, customs, and identity.

Disapproval at work is a manifestation of feeling rejected, both personally and professionally. It is the interruption of a mother's gaze that, in adulthood, unfolds as a professional conflict.

When Natalia felt ready to address her childhood wound in therapy, she realized that the company she worked for had not rejected her but rather, the innovative ideas she suggested, and her bosses were simply not prepared to develop them.

She then pursued a position at a multinational company based in her home country "with the idea of honoring my roots, true self, and reconnecting with everything I left behind," as she described overcoming her wound. In this way, the longing for home and country that had left her with a sense of desolation turned into a desire to strengthen her love for her birthplace.

The following are examples of childhood emotional wounds and some of the ways they are experienced in adulthood:

- **Rejection wound:** A person experiences the pain of not being accepted as they are and resorts to isolation, hiding, or fleeing from situations that evoke that emotion.
- **Abandonment wound:** It implies an emotional or physical absence from authority figures, and the protective measure consists of doing everything possible to avoid loneliness, thus leading to submitting to self-destructive relationships or bonds.
- **Humiliation or shame wound:** The person experiences invalidation, so they nullify their own needs and focus on fulfilling those of others.

- **Injustice wound:** It occurs when authority figures overlook the person's emotions, leading them to protect themselves by hiding what they feel and avoiding all forms of commitment for fear of judgment.
- **Disloyalty or betrayal wound:** The person has experienced lack of support from important figures, leading them to resort to control to ensure they are not betrayed.

Regardless of the cause of the wound and its history, it will have to travel the same path: honoring it to be able to release it. By accepting what has happened to cause the pain, we can move forward in life and seek to create space for new memories. We can always resort to the exercise of Once upon a Time whenever we feel a lack of freedom as a result of our childhood wounds and their echoes. This way, we will have the power to change the words in the narratives we tell ourselves and transition from a memory of suffering to one of healing.

# 3

# THE ISLAND GIRL WITH THE BOW AND ARROW

*This Is Us* is a TV series that accurately showcases the different facets of the emotional wound. Beth, one of the protagonists, is married to Randall and is director of the Philadelphia Ballet.

In her childhood, she aspired to be a professional dancer. Her father referred to her as a special girl who would one day change the world, his "little island girl who learned to dance before she could walk." He recalled an anecdote where the one-and-a-half-year-old was at a party, could not walk yet, and upon hearing the music, lifted her legs and danced directly toward him.

Beth's dreams were interrupted by her father's death and also by being replaced in her lead role in the school play, as her ballet teacher found another girl more suitable and qualified than her. This wound accompanied her into adulthood. As the director of the ballet, she focuses on selecting those dancers who "have that passion in their eyes" and remind her of her youth.

During a performance, one of her students falls to the ground, and Beth enters the stage to sit beside her as the audience watches. She encourages her to get up and continue.

Randall, sitting with their daughters, says: "There will be many things you won't remember about your mother, but you must never forget this. She is an extraordinary woman."

After the performance, Beth reaches out to the ballet teacher who rejected her in her youth.

He still remembered her and asked, "How are you?"

"Actually, I'm doing very well. I am the director of recruitment and development at the Philadelphia Ballet."

The teacher says, "What's the reason for your call?"

"I want to tell you that I was with you every day, and during my formative years you were my sun and my moon. To be honest, you were like a God to me . . . and it meant a lot that you chose me among the others to play the lead role within the ballet. . . . The trust you had in me was everything.

"I wanted to be your star, but when my father died and I couldn't dance at the level you required, you simply pushed me aside and replaced me with someone else, without a word of consolation or explanation. You didn't look back.

"When I think of that failure, my stomach turns, I find myself on an emotional roller coaster. It's the part of me that made me feel small; it's the part of me that I tried to hide from my husband and daughters; it's the part of me that I hated.

"I thought I would dance on the world's biggest stages, yet I learned that there is strength in supporting others, in being there for the dancers who are stars and those who are not. For a long time, I separated a part of myself, but no longer . . . . I am the island girl who danced before she could walk, and you took that from me, and now I will reclaim it. I know who I am, and I know what I should have done and couldn't."

This powerful passage shows the depth and intensity with which an emotional wound can settle in the psyche and erode a person's life, as well as the long process required to release it.

For Beth, the rejection from her teacher, along with her father's death and the loss of her sense of being the "island girl who danced before she could walk" led to the collapse of how she perceived her identity and place in the world. Since childhood, her father's voice telling the story of the little island girl who danced before she could walk was the fuel that ignited her self-esteem and the feeling of being cherished by those she loved so dearly.

After her father's death, Beth lost certainty in her value, and this was confirmed when her teacher chose to take her leading role away and replace her. Dancing not only represented her connection with her father but also the meaning her life held, and upon losing it, she identified with what she had lost: the belief that she was special and would change the world.

The emotional wound is, then, the loss of personal value, of what we cherish in ourselves that makes us feel unique and precious. Beth reconnects with her island girl when she realizes that no one has the power to take away her identity. It took her many years of hiding from herself by identifying with her wound, mourning, and losing her essence.

Reclaiming the purity of what we once believed about ourselves, a valuable perception of our being without fractures, is the path to honoring our need to let go. A beautiful representation is when Beth reconnects with her abandoned island girl by lifting a student up. By doing so, she transcends and redefines her painful past by providing the support she never received. In this manner, her abandonment wound is embraced when she chooses to stand by the young dancer, as if both of them were leaving the desert island together.

## It Is Time to Leave This Island

Greek mythology is filled with tragedies. It gives us a wide range of emotions that emerge from wounds caused by abandonment, betrayal, rejection, and any action that threatens the essence of humanity.

The play *Philoctetes* is a tragedy written by Sophocles that narrates the last year of the Trojan War. It focuses on topics like disability, loyalty, truth, lies, and forgiveness—elements that relate to emotional wounds—and was intended to foster the Greeks' sense of duty during times of war.

Philoctetes was a respected soldier who was famous for the bow and arrows given him by Heracles. During the Trojan War, he commanded seven ships but was expelled from the army due to a wound caused by a snake bite. He was abandoned on the island of Lemnos for 10 years due to the screams and cries caused by his pain, which affected the soldiers' concentration.

According to an oracle, Troy could only be taken with Heracles' bow and arrow, so Odysseus and Neoptolemus went to the island to convince Philoctetes to return to battle. He was healed and ended up killing Paris, the Trojan prince, with an arrow. After the conquest of Troy, Philoctetes founded several cities in Italy and assisted the people of the Greek island of Rhodes when natives attacked them.

Returning to the emotional wound—Philoctetes' tragedy is a representation of physical and emotional pain from abandonment. His solitary and painful journey, from Sophocles' viewpoint, is a pain that dignifies, a suffering that teaches and is experienced in solitude. It is a wound that turns the one who bears it into a hero and transcends the wound. When we have been deeply wounded, we suddenly find ourselves on a deserted island that is silent and terrifying. We scream in pain, but no one hears us. We fall, and no one sees us. That is how the wound feels.

Philoctetes says: "I had grown accustomed to my post, endured it as if in a dream, but today my eyes have been opened. Today, I awaken."

This line represents the awakening of consciousness in the face of abandonment as a revelation from which one cannot escape. This is why Philoctetes experiences a double wound. As he states, "The adversities I have suffered are too much; pain from the actions of those who were supposed to protect me."

Through their heroic acts, Beth and Philoctetes aim to dignify the wounds they have suffered over the years, feel compassion for themselves, and practice compassion toward others; the pain of others cannot be shared, but it can be validated and witnessed.

The snake bite wound Philoctetes suffers in his foot causes him physical torment that consumes him, but it also evokes an emotional ache of abandonment just as intense. After 10 years of relentless pain, he ends up identifying with the wound. His personality and self-perception are inseparable from his affliction.

Beth goes through the same with her teacher's rejection and the loss of her father. Both characters recognize and embrace their wounds when the pain has lessened, and they manage to "leave the island" where they were abandoned: She becomes the ballet director who helps students rise, and Philoctetes helps win the Trojan War.

Philoctetes says: "I will move forward. My past will not define me. The time has come to leave this island and never return."

The sublime pain of both stories allows us to understand how the wound can be healed by being seen and accepted as part of our vulnerability.

# 4

# EMOTIONAL INJURY AND POST-TRAUMATIC STRESS

It is important to differentiate between emotional injury and post-traumatic stress, as both concepts are often confused in clinical diagnoses when patients describe their symptoms.

Janina was on her honeymoon in New Orleans when Hurricane Katrina made landfall on August 29, 2005, with the force of a Category 3 cyclone. The massive, nine-meter-high waves flooded nearly 80 percent of the city, the drainage canals collapsed, and water escaped rapidly through the levees.

Thousands of residents were trapped without food and shelter. The chaos left by the flood disrupted all transportation, energy, water, sanitation, and medical services. Janina was staying in one of the slightly less affected areas, but a series of shocking experiences she had never lived through before led her to subsequently develop significant post-traumatic stress.

The day before Hurricane Katrina arrived, Janina and her husband tried to rent a car to leave the city but found that they could not, as all rental vehicles were taken and public transportation was also overwhelmed. On their way back to the hotel, they stopped to buy canned food in a store, where people were swarming the shelves and there were already looting incidents. On their return to their hotel, they realized that the water had been cut off, which made them think that the situation was going to worsen and that they needed to find another way to escape the danger.

Some hotels transported their guests to the Superdome, where authorities intended to evacuate them in trucks out of the city; however, the trucks never arrived, and by the next day, they and over 10,000 other people were trapped in the stadium by the hurricane and had to stay put for several days.

Conditions were deplorable. There was flooding, accumulating garbage, no water or food, no bathrooms or sufficient sleeping places, people were sick, and the smell of decomposition was overpowering. Despite the circumstances, a week later, Janina managed to send a text message to her cousin in New Orleans to let her know she was at the Superdome.

One of the volunteers in charge of maintaining order and distributing water remembered Janina and her husband due to their heavy Latino accents and the despair and uncertainty they displayed as they asked where they should set up their things in the Superdome. This is how the young volunteer managed to reunite Janina with her cousin, who had gone to look for them while the volunteer was organizing the cleaning crews at the stadium entrance. Finally, the newlyweds arrived at Baton Rouge Airport to catch a flight back to Mexico City.

Post-traumatic stress is a psychological disorder that appears in individuals after they experience or witness a terrifying event and prevents recovery from its impacts. The disorder can last for months or years, during which time people experience intense episodes of anxiety whenever they recall the catastrophic event. This leads to intense emotional and physical reactions, such as nightmares, overreaction to certain stimuli, or depression, triggered by recurrent memories of the event.

Janina started therapy six months after surviving Katrina, as she had a recurring nightmare in which a pile of garbage, mud, and people were crushing her. At night, she would wake up with a racing heartbeat and shortness of breath, which prevented her from falling asleep due to the intense fear generated by those images. The lack of sleep caused anxiety, desperation, and the need to flee from crowded places and avoid interpersonal relationships with family and friends. (People who suffer a traumatic event are very likely to experience reactions like nightmares, anxiety, depression, and the need to avoid situations or contexts that trigger memories of the event.)

Therapy for cases like this entails breaking down the traumatic event into sections, or steps. This helps the patient slowly approach the terrifying experience from a safe and contained place. This "safe and contained place" is the present moment, from which vantage point they can observe the past experience, along with the thoughts and sensations that are causing distress in the body, and realize that the danger no longer exists.

The therapeutic intervention I conducted with my patient consisted of discussing her nightmare over several sessions, each time including a scene or image with her narration, as well as making drawings of the terrifying elements and symbols from the dream.

We focused on those elements that paralyzed her or triggered anxiety, and we practiced a sequence of breaths I had previously taught her. This conscious breathing exercise was crucial in dissolving her post-traumatic stress and is also highly effective in returning to the present moment when we feel overwhelmed or invaded by childhood wounds.

The exercise involves inhaling air through the nose and exhaling through the mouth in three steps:

1. Inhale deeply through the nose.
2. Hold the oxygen between the throat and chest.
3. Exhale through the mouth.

The three steps are done for the same number of seconds as the inhalation. For example, if we inhale for 5 seconds, we also hold for 5 seconds and exhale for 5 seconds. It is an effective exercise that is carried out for 3 minutes to reduce anxiety and return to the present moment.

We only breathe in the present; in breathing there is no past or future. The present moment is the only evidence we have that we are alive or that we have survived a tragic event. It is the only moment when we can take control of our lives or make different choices. It is the moment from which we can rescue ourselves. This way, the brain oxygenates and the anxious thoughts weaken. In fact, all techniques aimed at placing us in the present moment are effective for healing emotional wounds. Several of them are included in the second part of the book.

After a few months, Janina managed to reduce her insomnia and rejection of social contexts and later joined a group of volunteers to work with people who have been victims of natural disasters.

I had the opportunity to work with Rocío, who experienced a traumatic event during the 2017 earthquake in Mexico City.

She ran out of her building to go to her son's kindergarten a few blocks away. From the corner, she saw that the place had collapsed. During the few seconds it took her to get there, she thought of all the possible scenarios of a life without her son. Fortunately, that didn't happen, as the children had been evacuated and were safe.

Nevertheless, terror invaded her so deeply that she never returned to her building, moved to another neighborhood, rented a house, hired a moving company to pick up her furniture, changed her son's school, and for almost a year had the earthquake alert app activated on her phone. We worked together for a year so she could regain inner peace, lessen her destruction fantasies, and regain the confidence to go to public places.

## Post-Traumatic Stress and Emotional Injury

While post-traumatic stress is defined by an event that jeopardizes life, emotional injury only occurs in childhood and can develop from a subtle, almost unnoticed situation or gain strength through a violent experience. In both cases, the wound digs into the psyche in such a way that the child confuses themselves with the pain they experience and feels inadequate or unworthy of receiving love.

Post-traumatic stress is directed at a particular event and is usually unexpected; emotional injury can include a series of experiences that mean the same thing for the patient, such as rejection or abandonment; in adulthood, these experiences may occur at work, in a romantic relationship, or in their personal projects, to mention a few triggers.

In the next chapter, we will discuss wounds that originate in childhood. Everything that hurts in the years that follow is merely an echo of the original wound.

# 5

# ONLY IN CHILDHOOD

In her book *The Soul Bird*, Israeli journalist, editor, and poet Michal Snunit offers a beautiful metaphor that describes the relationship between the outer world of our being and the inner world of our soul, where a bird resides that is responsible for opening and closing the drawers of our feelings.

To know this inner world, we must pay attention to the bird's messages and listen; we must recognize how the outer world influences our emotions.

The child looks for a mirror in the outside world to see themselves, feel validation, and confirm who they are. I used the word "confirm" for a reason. The child does not doubt themselves; it is the contrast with their surroundings that makes them do that. We were not born emotionally broken but became fractured over time. The child is spontaneous and naïve, with reactions that are aimed at meeting their immediate needs; that is, obtaining what gives them pleasure and connects them to the flow of life.

In the first stage of development, especially up to age seven, the brain is permeable and absorbs all available stimuli, from temperature, the tone of others' voices, looks, to love, rejection, loneliness, abandonment, and the comfort of a hug. It is now known that a child's learning ability is strengthened when they feel seen, receive physical and visual contact, and perceive the tenderness and warmth of the mother or any loving figure in charge of them and providing security and protection.

It is important to note that the feminine element nurtures and creates the container for the baby to develop. Any figure that expresses this feminine energy, whether father, uncles, grandparents, or a nanny, can provide the emotional support the child needs. Just as Mother Earth nurtures and gives life, it is the mother who injects the child with vitality. When a child is deprived of these identity-affirming elements, they feel confused and disoriented, without a mirror in which to look at themselves.

It is important to mention that it is not my intention to blame parents but to explain the singularity of the child's world, in order to have a gentle understanding of what may have happened in our childhood, even if it was a happy one.

Some families have a cordial, loving, and collaborative dynamic, so in such cases, the childhood wound occurs unexpectedly. It may be triggered by the parents' expectation that their children will maintain family stability, follow the same path as their careers or family businesses, or by too many aspirations that are hard to fulfill. Perhaps the pressure the child feels to maintain the qualities for which they are valued in the family, such as intelligence, beauty, or joy, is another reason to connect with the wound.

So, will the childhood wound appear anyway? Yes, but it is true that there are more complicated childhoods than others, and some people find it harder to overcome the difficulties of adult life.

According to French neurologist and psychiatrist Boris Cyrulnik, in his book *Psychoecology: The Environment and the Seasons of the Soul*, childhood is the stage where the conditions and limitations are generated predicting how we will face life. The connections we establish at the beginning of life set the tone for how we manage adversity later on and the level of resilience we can draw on. Cyrulnik defines resilience as the way we recover after a traumatic psychic agony and resume life after the pain that has impacted us.

In the first years of life, our parents or authority figures represent an extension of ourselves, there is virtually no differentiation between the baby's body and the mother's until the child begins to sit up and, most particularly, crawl. That is why the image of the child moving away from the mother and turning back to see that she is still there is so touching.

## Naming a Slippery Thought Out Loud

In my private practice, I use a highly effective exercise I call Naming a Slippery Thought Out Loud, which trains the patient to pay attention to their thoughts throughout the day and ask themselves, *Who do these words I just said sound like?* After a couple of days, patients can differentiate very clearly the voices that do not belong to them that have been implanted in the depths of their beings for many years.

I practice these exercises myself, not only to experience firsthand what patients go through but also because they have helped me evolve in my own personal process. The more I pay attention to my thoughts, the more the voices of my father or mother differentiate from mine, and that is when I manage to connect with my own voice.

This is quite an effective exercise, as the thoughts our parents have about us are the fuel of our wound. Here are two I have discovered in my own inner world:

- *Who are you to change the world? You are not Mother Teresa of Calcutta thinking you can help others.* Discovering my father's voice in my thoughts allowed me to let go of the hurt of not considering myself valuable and my father's rejection of the most luminous thing within me: helping people change the world.
- My mother used to tell me that women have to endure men's infidelity: *There's nothing you can do about it.* For several years, my mother's phrases led me to choose partners who were unfaithful or with whom I felt insecure in using my own voice. It was not until I broke up with a boyfriend who psychologically abused me, and undertook a long therapeutic process, that I could set aside my mother's voice and seek healthier relationships.

Adrián had learning difficulties during elementary school. He was easily distracted, and his classmates made fun of him when the teacher asked him a question.

Years later, he wanted to pursue a degree, but his father opposed it. He considered Adrián a poor student, without the necessary intelligence to achieve his dream, so he hid the books Adrián used to study for his university admission exam.

One afternoon, his father caught Adrián hiding something behind his back and confronted him.

"What are you hiding?" he asked.

"It's just a book," Adrián said.

"You're a fraud. I don't believe you!" his father shouted while pushing him.

It took several years of therapeutic work for Adrián to clear that phrase from his mind and quit addictions and his need to hide from the world.

Óscar told me that during his childhood, he was fascinated by art and school plays. At seven years old, during a family meal, he proudly recited the lines of the main character in a play, a role he had been given by his teacher. The adults started laughing and making fun of him. This went on for about a year. As a result, he isolated himself from his peers, refused to take part in the play, and his love for art disappeared. Over time, he became an aggressive child.

Twenty years later, Óscar came to therapy to resolve a dilemma: whether to continue working in his father's family business or study a profession related to art. The loyalty and love he had for his family were enough reasons to give up his artistic dreams and work within the family business to meet his father's expectations of continuing the family legacy.

Childhood phrases spoken by adults in his life still echo in Óscar's mind as though they are his own words, making it difficult for him to find his own voice and make a decision. His lack of vitality and rigidity in showing his emotions bespeak his childhood fear of rejection and sadness at feeling alone.

Óscar experiences what we all go through at some point in life: sacrificing our essence in order to belong. But he has found a life opportunity to work on his emotional wound—he is currently studying for a master's degree in film.

## The Analyst's Compulsion

Alice Miller, a Polish psychoanalyst recognized for her work on child abuse and its effects on the individual and society, explains how during childhood, affective needs and intense feelings of anger, distress, fear, and pain are repressed in order to earn the affection and acceptance of the parents. The child adopts a behavior according to what they believe is expected of them, thereby annihilating their own personality. When they accept the role others want them to play, this leads to a loss of identity.

Miller's studies focused on the consequences of World War II on the children who lived through it. She found that those with a high intellectual quotient and significant emotional burden, due to a challenging environment or having authoritarian and possessive parents, developed the ability to sacrifice themselves to please and compensate for their parents' deficiencies and frustrations.

In this way, the child becomes the child the parents expect them to be, and it is this "ideal" child they want and accept, not the true being that is their child.

Through this sacrifice, the child becomes a little adult who takes on responsibilities that are not their own. They do all they can to provide comfort to their parents by setting aside their own needs, eliminating attitudes of rebellion or expressing negative feelings, and avoiding being pampered or considered.

Such parents are mainly focused on themselves and stop emotionally nurturing their child. Their child then grows into an adult who seeks the acceptance of others by knowing what is expected of them; they also develop the ability to understand the minds of others in order to meet their expectations and strengthen the bond. The problem arises when the person gets tired of pretending to be someone else to obtain the acceptance and love of those they have tried to keep satisfied despite their own affective needs.

Emotional or affective needs are related to everything that strengthens our self-esteem and gives us security, knowing that we are accepted for who we really are. Affective needs are generally related to seeking connections or situations that reduce stress, fear, and the feeling of loneliness. This is why we often prefer to "please" and set aside these needs to maintain the connection, rather than asking for what we truly need. We prefer to be loved by others even if it means our own silence, self-sacrifice, and betraying ourselves. The illusion of having achieved a relationship in which we feel validated fades as soon as we try to use our authentic voice to ask for our affective needs to be met.

*New Amsterdam* is an American TV medical drama series based on Eric Manheimer's book *Twelve Patients: Life and Death at Bellevue*

*Hospital*. One of the characters displaying the scars of childhood wounds is Dr. Lauren Bloom, head of the Emergency Department at New Amsterdam Medical Center. The plot reveals that Dr. Bloom is addicted to Adderall, a drug used to treat attention deficit disorder, which hinders her work performance and generates conflicts with her colleagues. At one point, she seeks help to address her addiction and enters a rehabilitation program.

During Lauren's childhood, her mother drank too much alcohol at the parties she hosted at home, and when they ended, she would complain and become a violent woman. Finally, she would vomit until she passed out, at which point, the daughter would take care of cleaning her mother up and putting her to bed. She felt it was her responsibility to take care of her, as her father remained indifferent, absent from home, and sought refuge in his work, leaving Laura in charge of what happened at home, and effectively, leaving her to her own devices.

Lauren learned to justify her father's absence, to be empathetic toward him, and to deny her negative emotions about his abandonment. She never asked her parents to meet her affective needs and assumed the role of protector for her mother.

A year before Lauren went to college, her father passed away, and she left home to escape her mother and go in search of a new life. But she felt guilty about leaving her teenage sister, who was addicted to heroin, and her mother who continued consuming alcohol.

Sometime later, she reunited with her mother and tried to address her childhood wound:

"Do you know what my first memory is? I was seven years old, and I drank your martini thinking that if I did, it could stop you from doing it. But you poured another glass and yelled at me—not for finding me drunk but for dirtying the floor. I spent years angry with you, hating you, and feeling compassion until I stopped feeling anything for you. I was just a child trying to get close to you. You were an adult, and you didn't even try, and it makes me sad because you did me wrong. It's terrible because I didn't deserve it. Just tell me you're sorry so I can go."

"I wish I could. I want to, and I regret that you're sad. But, dear, I don't remember any of that happening," her mother said.

# I Suppose This Is the Worst That Has Happened to You . . .

I agree with the title of Alice Miller's book *The Drama of the Gifted Child: The Search for the True Self*—the drama of childhood definitively lies in the fact that the child realizes that to survive certain family situations, they have to sacrifice themselves, forget their emotional needs, and satisfy their parents' expectations.

It is for this reason that in my treatment, I focus on establishing an emotional channel with the patient that allows them to validate their true desires, claim their rights, and talk about those times where they felt betrayed or alone and could not express it at the time. This is a process of recovering their dignity, which allows them to take ownership of their story and create new meaning from their childhood wound by finding those things worth living for.

At the beginning of any therapeutic process, it is common to hear patients justifying their parents' actions; blaming themselves for deserving punishment or not receiving love due to their way of being, dreams, or needs; and considering themselves to be not worthy, too demanding or too much to handle. This reflects the distance they feel from what truly matters to them and what their parents think is inappropriate.

Another form of resistance to the healing path consists of minimizing traumatic experiences or forgetting humiliating and abusive situations.

After two years of therapy, Diana remembered that her mother used to borrow her dresses, which she would cut to fit because she was taller than her daughter, and also that she would use her makeup. She would burn her expensive clothes as well. For Diana, recognizing her mother's destructive intentions was painful, so she feigned indifference when talking about her memories.

It was not until I expressed indignation that she allowed herself to feel the anger she had repressed for many years. "How could your mother dare do something like that?" I asked.

When we are children, we wish to keep our parents' image intact at all costs, so, in order not to lose them, we take on their guilt as though we are the ones who are flawed. We choose to admire and respect them in spite of everything.

Another supportive function I provide is that I create a voice that expresses what they have kept silent, allowing them to question and explore a range of emotions around the suppressed childhood wound. I select some phrases or words with strong connotations that question what they have narrated, at times using a third-person voice expressing something like: "How awful!" "It's incredible to hear this," "How terrible!"

There are occasions when I ask direct questions with a dual purpose of inquiring what the patient feels or thinks about it and making a disguised affirmation: "Do you realize this fact is unacceptable, right?" "Is it safe to assume this is the worst that has happened to you?"

## Contrasting My Approach

In traditional treatments like psychoanalysis, the therapist is supposed not to judge or give any opinion regarding the patient's narrative. Basically, the methodology consists of the patient lying on a treatment couch and facing the ceiling and speaking. It is a method of soul (psyche) investigation that generally uses four working tools:

1. **Free Association** – This is a technique established by Sigmund Freud, an Austrian physician and neurologist and founder of psychoanalysis, in which the patient verbally expresses all thoughts and ideas that come to mind spontaneously in order to establish new connections and release what has been repressed.
2. **Floating Attention** – The therapist listens in order to recognize all elements included in the patient's tale without passing judgment on them.
3. **Analysis and Management of Transference with Regard to the Relationship between the Patient and the Analyst** – Transference occurs as a result of the patient's unconscious attitudes toward the therapist, who symbolizes an authority figure, typically from the past; countertransference is the

therapist's own reaction to these attitudes. Countertransference is the emotional response and conscious or unconscious reactions of the therapist projected onto the patient. For example, the therapist may feel anger or frustration over the patient's attitudes, attracted to or identified with the patient, or anxiety or fear about their experiences. It is important for the therapist to be aware of their own emotional reactions and to use them to better understand the patient, rather than allowing them to interfere with the therapeutic process.

4. **Interpretation** – The therapist intervenes and explains to the patient the meaning of these unconscious attitudes.

The goal of this methodology is for the patient to discover by themselves the unconscious aspects that bind them to their past. Here, the analyst remains silent throughout the session and does not react to what the patient expresses. Occasionally, they offer an interpretation. In traditional psychoanalysis, patient memories may be influenced by fantasies of aggression or pleasure and the defense mechanisms to repress them. Memories are considered an unconscious elaboration rather than a clear, true memory of what occurred. In my methodology, I accompany patients in the memories they narrate and validate their perceptions.

From my perspective, approaching memory as fantasy can confuse the patient and make them doubt themselves. There are cases of consciously or unconsciously invented memories, but for me these are irrelevant, since I work with what is presented and what the patient offers me: whether they are telling the truth, believe it, or invent it. In my case, the therapeutic intention is to reach consciousness through the path they themselves propose in order to pursue the opportunity for healing. Reflecting on how this past truth impacted their life will allow them to recognize the voice of their present.

To address the problem, a therapeutic relationship must be established that can create the most favorable conditions for the patient to let go of that moment in their development when they were disturbed by an emotional wound. This allows their authentic personality to emerge in the here-and-now, so that they can express their natural selves as purely as possible. In these new scenarios, the patient has a healthier response to traumatic memories from their past.

During our conversations, in my role as therapist, I react with anger, indignation, amazement, or any other emotion over actions of abuse or mistreatment that were directed at them. This tool allows space for the pain of that childhood wound to emerge, against which, for various reasons, they could not defend themselves.

## Stop, Recognize and Honor, and Heal

Creating space in consciousness to feel the pain is necessary. It may be that the patient has never felt indignant about their treatment, as they were prohibited from experiencing the emotion in childhood or made to believe that the mistreatment they received was normal.

Lourdes casually told me that her mother locked the room, leaving her alone with her father when she was only seven. He asked her to undress and took photos of her, which he later developed and pasted on the closet wall. He would then show them to her, saying that he did that to admire her beauty.

"My father admired me a lot," she said.

At that moment, I expressed indignation and judged her parents' actions to be child pornography and abuse. Lourdes reacted with amazement. It was as if a veil had been pulled back from in front of her eyes. She suddenly understood where her recurring nightmares were coming from—being naked in a dark room and unable to leave.

For patients to love the child they once were, they need to be accepted for their authentic emotions. As a therapist, I believe it is essential to create an atmosphere of protection, empathy, and respect so that the patient can feel accompanied and confident about speaking their truth. I do not consider it healthy or healing to remain neutral to accounts of childhood wounds. On the contrary: If we witness and accompany that pain, validating those terrible experiences of suffering, we can comfort the child within them and discover who they truly are.

As Alice Miller says in *The Body Never Lies: The Lingering Effects of Cruel Parenting*: "True adulthood would mean no longer denying the truth. It would mean feeling the repressed suffering, consciously acknowledging the story remembered by the body at an emotional level, and integrating that story instead of repressing it."

## The Embrace of a Voice

Another voice I include and consider the most powerful is the one representing feminine elements like empathy, containment, warmth, shelter, and unconditionality. I verbalize feelings of helplessness, such as abandonment, loneliness, rejection, shame, and humiliation that the patient experienced but kept to themselves.

Here, their body language is crucial if I am to know whether I am connecting with the experiences that installed the emotional wound. I use phrases such as "You must have felt terribly alone," "That must have been very painful," "You took responsibility for something that wasn't yours," "It's time to take care of yourself."

Once the patient is accustomed to recognizing a voice of self-care in their narrative and has started to use words that convince them that they deserve to validate their painful experience, I then introduce a new voice, which I call the Analytical Voice. It is the voice of me, as their therapist.

## The Analytical Voice

The Analytical Voice speaks in the first person and in the present tense. I draw analogies between the traumatic experience of childhood and current adulthood situations where the patient can clearly see the impact the wound has on their reactions. In this way, I anticipate, alongside them, scenarios that could trigger the pain from the past allowing them to choose an adult response instead of experiencing childhood desolation.

For example, for a person who experienced abandonment and took on responsibilities at a noticeably young age, and who in adulthood becomes an authority figure in a family, emotional triggers happen when they must deal with multiple tasks leading them to feel the loneliness of their past. When tired or unable to fulfill their duties, they get angry, anxious, and fearful of losing control. Consequently, they isolate themselves and try to face the situation.

So, in the Analytical Voice, I use phrases like: "Remember that you must ask for help in these moments; if you don't, you will feel abandoned again," "Remember that you shouldn't keep these emotions to yourself."

In this way, a therapeutic alliance is formed, where the person no longer feels alone; but above all, where their experiences, perceptions, and appreciation of what governs their life and what they oversee now in the present are validated.

## Touching the Soul

The therapeutic voice is one of many strategies I have used over the years to help the patient return to their essence, inner child, or soul, as Boris Cyrulnik, Gustav Carl Jung, and Mijal Snunit call this innocent and pure part of the personality.

While I was pursuing my Ph.D. in individual and couples psychotherapy at the Mexican Institute of the Couple, the director, Mariano Barragán, taught a technique called Touching the Patient's Soul. This technique involved placing the patient inside the Gesell Room, a chamber set up to observe people's behavior that was divided by one-way mirrored glass with a mirror on the side facing the observed individuals with their therapist, and other professionals on the opposite side, witnessing the process.

The technique involves performing a therapeutic intervention powerful enough to bring about a modification in the patient's body language, such as crying. Therapists had only five minutes to make this happen. After that time, almost always a phone would ring inside the room and on being picked up, Mariano's voice could be heard saying, "You have failed."

Back then, I didn't understand what "touching the soul" meant, much less how such a feat could be achieved. It took a couple of decades to discover what my director meant by "touching the soul."

It means connecting with the truth of the inner child. When you touch a person's soul, they experience a bodily sensation they can't control. They are overwhelmed by a nostalgia that can't be explained; tears just flow from an unexpected place in the unconscious. I used the word "nostalgia" because it precisely defines the feeling that something has been left behind, and despite the longing to recover it, one senses it will never be the same. "What has been lost" can mean endless things depending on each individual's experiences.

As a therapist, one knows when nothing relevant is happening in a session as opposed to when a significant connection has been made that shakes the patient's core. I am always on this quest. I must confess that when I touch someone's soul, it is not always planned. It arises in a decisive moment when a word, a sigh, an observation, or a silence suddenly make great sense, and the person feels like they have recovered something lost in childhood. Have you ever felt this?

Explosive crying has indicated that I have touched a patient's soul. But crying is not the only way of contacting the soul. It can be any intense emotion, including changes in gaze, changes in countenance, or even changes in body posture.

I remember I once said to Angélica: "It must be exhausting for you not to receive your father's love and attention."

She didn't say a word, her eyes welled up, and she continued sobbing for the next half hour of the session. I remained silent all that time, simply watching. At the end, she asked if she could have a hug.

Did I give it to her? Of course I did! This is what I mean by ceasing to be neutral. Her inner child needed the hug she had never received and asked for it from her adulthood; denying it would immediately have taken her back to the original wound.

Hugging a patient is a controversial act in the psychoanalytic approach, but as I mentioned, neutrality leaves the patient adrift. This doesn't mean I go around hugging patients, but there are various forms of active accompaniment, such as true listening, the therapist's objection or indignation at their suffering, or the appreciation of their qualities that were previously ignored. There are countless ways to connect with people's souls.

Shared laughter also proves to be a highly effective tool to alleviate pain and feel supported. My patients and I have laughed a lot about moments in their lives that were once unbearable.

One patient suffered a lot because his wife went to a bar with friends once a week, creating feelings of abandonment in him. These feelings were akin to those he experienced as a child, when his mother lied to him about where she was going and went out to play cards with friends, leaving him alone at home. For six months, he talked about the same issue, saying that his wife didn't even bother to make dinner for him before leaving.

In one of those sessions, I said: "What about if you make yourself one of those instant soups and stop waiting for her?"

For a few seconds, he looked at me seriously, as if I had suggested something unimaginable, and then burst out laughing and replied: "That's what it has been about. No more waiting!"

This is another way to connect with the soul—proposing something that appears irrelevant but has enough of an impact to offer a way out of a situation that hurts too much.

Why soup?

Because aromas trigger pleasant or unpleasant memories. A home that smells of food represents in the unconscious a sense of nourishment and care. For my patient, making his own soup meant emotionally nurturing himself and feeling the warmth of home that his inner child never received. He stopped waiting for his mother's love and that of his wife. He is divorced and now lives on his own, happily cooking different recipes.

## Let's Play

Another way of accessing the inner child's soul, I have discovered, is to investigate which activities excite the patient the most, whether they actually have performed them at different points in their life, or not. Generally, these are activities they keep secret or dream of doing someday. Just as children know how to sacrifice themselves in order to be loved, seen, or validated, they also are clear on what they find fascinating and invigorating. Our inner child is that part of us that knows what makes us happy and is always waiting for us, as adults in our present moment, to bring it to reality.

When that inner voice is active, we feel inspired and have a sensation of timelessness, a desire for it to never end. Inspiration comes from "the spirit that dwells within us"; that is, a part of us larger than our intellect that connects us to life, moves us, and brings us joy.

Inspiration is the door that opens to personal creativity. When a child doesn't have to worry about surviving conflicts in their environment, they develop their creative instinct through play and imagination. This is why children can play for hours without realizing it; time has no limits, and enlightenment serves its purpose.

When a child interrupts their creative process because of overwhelming family stress, then the encouraging or motivating voice becomes silent or dull, allowing them to be alert and to defend themselves.

Still, our inner child's voice persists throughout our lives, asking us not to abandon our inspiration and that which connects us to life. With adulthood, we become serious, rushed, distracted, and anxious; we drift away from the child's voice that asks us to pause, enjoy, extend the excitement of time, and feel connected to something greater than ourselves.

It's a voice that tells us: "Let's play. Let's do what we love."

But as adults, we respond: "I can't right now. I have responsibilities. Maybe tomorrow."

The inner child trusts us and always waits for us, holding onto the hope that we will return to that vital place where time stops and connects us with the universe, but there comes a moment when it grows tired of waiting. When we postpone what inspires us or leads us on an adventure, the child's voice becomes sad. Just as we repress painful memories, we also do the same with those things we longed for that made us enthusiastic in childhood.

When our inner child's voice grows tired of waiting, the adult doesn't know what life goals to set or what activities they are passionate about.

On one occasion, I met a patient who wasn't interested in anything. When I tried to inquire about the reason, her response was consistent: "It doesn't hold my interest." "I'm not interested." "It doesn't excite me." "It means nothing to me."

She was a healthy woman, with a profession, a job, and sound financial status, yet she struggled to find a partner. I realized her inner voice was dormant. For a while, I focused on her desire to find a partner, but unfortunately, I discovered that what truly motivated her was the impossibility of being happy and apathy toward everything. Therapy represented a place where she confirmed that nothing could change, and that I, as her therapist, only served as a witness to her prophecy. In short: I couldn't help her.

Over the years, I have met some patients who arrive at my office "soulless or disenchanted"; that is, they feel disconnected from themselves and cannot feel any emotion that connects them to their true desires. In such cases, I have been unable to implement the usual strategies that work with a little willingness on both sides. The pain these patients have experienced has been so impactful that their inner world has become inert, anesthetized. When I find myself wishing for a fulfilling life for a patient more than they desire it for themselves, it is time to let go.

It doesn't usually take long for me to connect with patients and for us to embark on the adventures of their inner child, even with those who arrive depressed, fearful, angry, anxious, and distrustful. There comes a moment when they extend their hand for you to accompany them in exploring their true selves. A wide range of possibilities opens up to work through the pain they have endured.

In this way, I support them in validating their experience and the emotions tied to it, allowing them to build paths of trust that enable them to connect with themselves and with those parts they have forgotten. There are different techniques to connect with the true self, which I will mention in the second part of the book.

## Life Plan

The expectations and wishes that parents have for their children's lives are filled with good intentions. They genuinely believe that if they design a life plan for their children's future, they won't suffer and will achieve their goals. However, the plans parents have for their children can paradoxically be the origin of their emotional wounds in many cases.

It is a natural to think about things we want for our children when planning their future: family values, a school that aligns with the standard of education in the home, professions we believe to be prominent, our own view of success, aspects of life we find valuable and those we do not, moral values that should be upheld, marriage and children (or not), the appropriate sexual orientation, and a myriad of other criteria.

Certainly, we need a structure in education to guide, care for, and provide support as a form of love in action. But how do we know the fine line between giving them tools for growth and blocking our children's true expression? It's a difficult question to answer. Perhaps we could start by questioning if some of the decisions we've made have been geared towards our well-being, fulfilling our own frustrated dreams, or more so, confronting our fears through our children.

I experienced this dilemma when my son finished high school. To me, it was an exciting time. I love studying, and despite having two master's degrees and a doctorate and completed numerous courses and diplomas, I still feel like life is too short to learn everything I desire.

I had several conversations with my son in the months before he graduated and suggested that a film degree seemed ideal for him, as I consider him a creative and sensitive young man. He agreed and studied for the admission exam at a university I also recommended to him. During this process, I took on the task of seeking out all of the schools and universities that offer film programs, reviewed their curricula, watched virtual campus tours, and even made a list of the pros and cons of each institution. At the end of this arduous research, I was so excited I even thought about pursuing a master's degree in film myself. Why not?

My son? He simply wasn't interested. I honestly believed that I was helping him by supporting him in pursuing a life career that I was (and still am) confident he would succeed in. He didn't pass the admission exam and didn't want to try again.

One afternoon, he sat down beside me and said: "Mom, I want you to know that I'm not going to study anymore. I don't like it the way you do, and I prefer to work."

My son has always been noticeably clear about who he is, but his love for me and desire not to disappoint me were enough for him to sacrifice. And for my part, I thought that what worked for me would do him good, too.

Releasing the expectation and idea I had of how his future should be took some time. My son taught me a great lesson: He decided to work. The path he chose, his own, allowed me to discover some of his qualities, including responsibility, humility, and commitment to what he enjoys. At times, I still have my doubts and wonder if I should not have insisted more.

My concerns were about whether parents should insist on higher education (almost to the point of forcing a child to study) because they believe it will ensure the child a better future, or whether they should let them follow their own path, even if they disagree with it. How far can one interfere in a child's destiny? Should I have done more? Should I have forced them to study? Some parents impose university education on a child as an obligation, due to family tradition, regardless of the child's opinion. To what extent can a family norm shape their path? Is respecting their "calling" or desire enough?

Perhaps part of my child's emotional wound is that I didn't trust him or couldn't see him. What remains for me to do is to honor his place in the world from where he wants to be.

I have heard many stories of patients who fear disappointing their parents, even losing their love, if they live a life different from their expectations. In some families, there is no room for children to choose their path; there are traditions and loyalties that are hard to break for the individual.

When I finished high school, I applied for an architecture degree with the hope that in the future, I could work alongside my father, who is a civil engineer. Throughout my life, I had tried to please him, and I thought that studying something related to his profession would make him happy. In my fantasy, it was another demonstration of my admiration for him.

Before entering university, I took a sabbatical year in Israel, where I had experiences that allowed me to feel more like myself, and my perspective changed. In that country, I realized that what truly sparked my passion was helping people, and the field of psychology largely reflected what my soul had been seeking. So, from a different continent, I made the determination to change my major and requested my parents to go along with the change.

My father never validated my profession; he didn't believe I could change the world. With a chuckle, he spoke those immortal words mentioned earlier: "You think you're Mother Teresa of Calcutta trying to help, as if that were possible."

There were many other aspects of my life he didn't like, and it was only when I let go of wanting him to love me that I achieved inner peace.

Barbara told me that her father handed her a life plan with a complete list of what she should do from age 15 to menopause. The goal was to provide her with steps to follow to be a good professional, meaning not getting married or having children, which was what she truly desired. During her adolescence, she secretly played housewife and mother and fantasized about a life she wanted so badly but was not accepted by her father.

Despite her father's wishes, Barbara married twice and had children. After several years of marriage, she was left a widow by her second husband and had to work to support her family. Her desire to be "just a housewife" was again thwarted by financial difficulties.

Resentment and anger toward her parents emerged in therapeutic work when she recognized the childhood wounds related to rejection, authoritarianism, and emotional abuse she had endured. On the one hand, she had suffered as a result of her father's control and lack of empathy; on the other, from her mother's silence. Her need to occupy a different place in her life and for her own voice to be heard led her to seek help. From this theme, we began to work on what place she desired to occupy in the world.

One way of maintaining control over children is by judging or criticizing their dreams or indicating that they won't be successful. So how do we strike a balance between providing them tools for their growth and safeguarding their true self's voice?

The answer lies in listening. However, it's not as simple as it appears. To truly see others, we need to do long-term personal work that involves self-awareness and hold ourselves accountable for our actions, strengthen humility, and practice respect. Only with this discipline in our lives can we forge deep connections with those we love.

To practice respect, we must strengthen our tolerance for frustration, identify the triggers that make us angry, pause to reflect on how we have hurt or embarrassed people, and understand how we need to exert control. It's a day-to-day effort, one with which we must be willing to engage. It's our duty to strive to be aware of our actions as well as our own wounds.

**Four Steps**

In my therapeutic practice, I have often guided patients in validating their painful experiences and healing the image they hold of their parents in their inner world, which is where the true healing can take place. This occurs through four steps and specific moments within therapy when we:

1. Recognize and validate our childhood wound experience and its emotional impact on our present life and accept what happened to us.
2. Allow repressed emotions such as anger, sadness, rejection, abandonment, shame, and loneliness to surface.
3. Reframe and build a healthy relationship with our parents in our inner world, letting go of the images of them that have been destructive.
4. Discover our truth and zest for life and learn to respect ourselves.

When we become conscious of our childhood reality while being witnessed in our pain by someone (either a therapist or a trusted individual), we stop repressing and denying this feeling and all its nuances. By attentively listening without judgment, we can observe all that we feel and recognize it with curiosity and gentleness. We can speak to ourselves lovingly, as we needed to be spoken to in the past, and understand and protect our emotions with the help of our new, self-compassionate voice.

# 6

# THE ARMOR

Robert Fisher's novel *The Knight in Rusty Armor* tells the story of a medieval knight who wore beautiful armor that reflected the sunlight when he went into battle and undertook heroic quests. The knight became so accustomed to his armor he never took it off, and his family forgot what his face looked like. One day, he decided to remove the armor, but found that he could not as it had melded to his body. The story unfolds as the man embarks on a quest to free himself from it.

This story vividly describes one of the main themes I've dealt with in my patients: the search for their true identity. Earlier, I mentioned how expectations from people around us (family, society, culture, and religion) deeply influence what we believe about ourselves and how we should behave in order to be seen and loved.

Our "emotional armor" is made up of the expectations, labels, and roles imposed on us by others, which we then internalize as our self-image. We construct this self-image from a young age, because we realize that if we wear this armor, we will be safe, accepted, and receive the love we desire. The messages we receive, especially from our parents, play a crucial role in forming this armor.

I recall that, from when I was very young, my father told me that I was "a good girl who never caused trouble," so that's how I behaved almost all my life. From elementary school through university, I was the favorite of many teachers, acquiescent to figures of authority. But "not causing trouble" stuck to my skin like the knight's armor and led to many other behaviors that harmed me, such as avoiding expressing my true emotions or thoughts, unintentionally keeping family secrets, and sacrificing my own desires for others' well-being. This behavior also extended to my friendships.

The armor seemingly protects us from suffering, but it distances us from who we truly are; its adaptive and survival functions make it hard for us to let go.

In recent years, I have carried out "acts of rebellion" that have led to the dissolution of my unconditionally obedient self-image and relationships with those who could not accept this more authentic version of me. "Being good" in my family system meant not questioning my parents or speaking about what happened at home, but most importantly, not having the right to set boundaries. Family expressions from childhood imprint on our unconscious minds to such an extent that as adults, we continue to strive to be someone we truly are not.

## Who Would You Be Without Your Story?

Byron Katie is a spiritual teacher who invites participants in her courses to question themselves through a series of specific questions that probe the thoughts shaping their life stories. As described in *Loving What Is: Four Questions that Can Change Your Life*, she employs a methodology she calls "The Work," which involves asking yourself four questions to help you identify distressing thoughts:

1. Is it true?
2. Can you absolutely know that it's true?
3. How do you react, what happens, when you believe that thought?
4. Who would you be without the thought?

Byron discovered that her suffering came from believing many of her thoughts, and she found relief when freeing herself from them. In essence, she realized that suffering was optional, and she asserts that this freedom is attained by reflecting on one's responses to the four questions. I too believe that this is a way to dismantle the armor and differentiate ourselves from what veils our true selves.

When we question the truth of what we tell ourselves, we can return to who we are and take responsibility for our actions. We then discover, that everything begins and ends in our minds, regardless of how events unfolded in the past. When we alter our perceptions, we free ourselves from others' expectations, expressions, and actions.

By being mindful of the distressing thoughts that cause us frustration, sadness, and anger, we can question and weaken their hold on us. This freedom is essential for exploring true identity and releasing the armor. It's a new adult perspective on the way we view the traumatic events of our past, but it is not an easy process. My patients have lived their stories for so long that it's hard for them to question them.

The emotional wound is the inevitable outcome of a traumatic event, but what's not inevitable is the way we come to define ourselves as a result of that trauma; that is, blaming and punishing ourselves or feeling unworthy as a result of what we experienced. Every time we view the world through our wound, we miss the opportunity to experience who we truly are.

One effective exercise I ask my patients to do is revisit the traumatic event in their imagination and look at it as the adult witnesses they are today. This fresh perspective helps them understand that, as children, they couldn't differentiate themselves from their pain.

Gerardo quit several jobs because he felt no one listened to him during work meetings. When I asked if this feeling resembled something from the past, he recalled family meals. He was the youngest of five siblings, and the only boy. His sisters wouldn't let him speak and ignored his requests for food at the table. When he was six years old, his mother wouldn't sit at the table as she was busy in the kitchen, while across from him was his father, who hid behind the newspaper he was reading and got up to watch the news before his children had finished eating.

After sharing his story, I asked him to narrate the event again from the perspective of an adult and neutral witness.

"Everyone was in their own world. It's not that the child wasn't worthy of being heard," he said while sitting on the couch in my office, watching that moment from his past as an outsider to his story.

Now, returning to the inevitability of the wound's occurrence: Was Gerardo ignored during family meals? Perhaps, but that's not the crucial question; rather, it is to carefully observe the conclusion we draw about ourselves based on a painful experience. These conclusions may cast doubt on a person's worth or the purpose of their existence, as my patient aptly described:

"From a very young age, I felt that I wasn't important to my family, that they didn't listen to me, because I was invisible to them, and I even felt that if I disappeared one day, no one would notice. Over time, I concluded I wasn't worthy and had no place in the world."

It's not the trauma affecting our lives but rather, what we believe about ourselves when the event occurred that leads to the emotional wound. If we could have reassured ourselves as children that there was nothing wrong with us, we wouldn't have to seek therapy as adults.

## *Sikhona* and *Sawubona*

One of the most beautiful aspects of childhood is the generosity with which children offer us their spontaneity. All of us who have had a child close by know the excitement with which they demand our attention when playing, painting, dancing, riding a tricycle, or running. Inevitably, we hear them say things like:

"Mom, watch me do this . . ." "See how nicely I did it . . ." "Did you like it?"

There are many varied ways of asking the world to look at us, validate us, and respect us. If you see me, I exist. If my existence matters to you, you love me. If you love me, I will never suffer. And if you do not see me, I do not exist, I do not matter to you, you do not love me, and I will suffer forever.

These premature conclusions can appear even at birth. An extraordinary spiritual teacher I know shared how she was emotionally affected by her father when she was born because he wanted a boy. Despite being a famous woman, author of several books, beloved by her students, partner, and friends, the conclusion of not belonging to this world has followed her throughout her life regardless of her success and the recognition she has received.

My father told me that after I was born, my mother had postpartum depression that lasted the first year and a half of my life, so she couldn't care for me, look at me, or even hug me. She was present as he told the story, did not object to what he was saying, nor try to justify herself, as if rejection were a normal condition within our family.

My conclusion about who I was in this world was affected for years. Thanks to the amount of personal work I have done I have managed to have a stable life, but the triggers of the wound are always there, whether it be the betrayal of a friend or when some of my professional projects do not receive the recognition I had expected.

When we discover the story we have created about our lack of worth or belonging in this world, an opportunity arises to stop, see what is happening to us, how we are judging ourselves based on the situation we experienced, and how we can find a healthier and more constructive meaning in the way we see ourselves. Through the practice of these reflections, we understand, over time, that our thoughts and emotions belong to us and that we can find the strength and freedom to resolve this.

For centuries, the Zulu community in South Africa has had the tradition of greeting each other with a kind of two-part invocation: *Sikhona*, which means "I am here to be seen," and *Sawubona*,[1] which means "I see you." The combination of these two words generates high-vibration emotions such as empathy, humility, respect, and generosity and also promotes honorability among people.

This is a simple and profound way of witnessing our own existence and that of the other, as well as being an act that affirms our presence. As children, we long for the *Sikhona* from our parents, and as adults, we seek the *Sawubona* when we decide to work on our healing process. How can we greet the world by affirming our presence?

## Invocation

An impactful therapeutic exercise I perform after six months treating my patients consists of remaining silent for five minutes and looking into each other's eyes. It is a deep connection that is established without words. Eye contact is another way to touch the soul and give a sense of unity, thereby generating the desire to establish honest communication.

---

[1] Cipri Quintas, *Sawubona: El secreto del verdadero éxito* (Alienta Editorial, 2022).

After the five minutes are over, my patient says, "I am here to be seen." And I respond, "I see you."

For three minutes, we alternate these phrases while looking into each other's eyes, and as we progress, the energy builds, and the invocation of our presences gains strength.

The Zulu people believe that the phrase "I am here to be seen" has the power to evoke the person's spirit presence. And saying "Here I am" is a declaration of our intention to fully inhabit this moment and indicates our willingness to commit with integrity. "To be seen" is an honest act emphasizing the absence of masks and armor, and it means: "This is who I am, and I will speak my truth."

"I see you" is a powerful experience for both the person saying it and the person hearing it. According to the Zulu tradition, saying "I see you" offers the intention to release any judgment and receive the person by seeing them as God created them. It is also an affirmation of our existence and the equality and respect that the person shows us.

This greeting represents the Zulu philosophy, which is a spiritual ethic that values the humanity of all people and advocates mutual support to give each other existence. It is an exercise that helps people remember their true identity, recognize their worth, and deeply engage with their being. It is in this practice that our best versions and those of others emerge.

The therapeutic process is, therefore, a psychological, spiritual, and emotional journey in which the patient can recognize themselves when they have ceased to identify with their past wound, have released their armor, and have rebuilt their inner world.

I consider this invocation so useful and meaningful that I invite all my patients to witness themselves, claim their place, and greet the world by affirming their presence.

# 7

# EXPIRATION DATE

Expiration dates are everywhere. Food and medication have deadlines for safe consumption, and after their expiration, it is advisable to avoid using them, as we could experience toxicity or reduced potency or side effects from out-of-date medications.

In a similar way, ill effects can happen with our out-of-date traumatic experiences and the emotions tied to them. While some people may be able to consume expired foods and medicines with no ill effects, others continue to experience emotions as intense as those they felt when their emotional wound first occurred.

It might seem negligent to consume something that can harm us or continue creating situations that provoke devastating emotions, but we usually have our own specific reasons for doing so.

When we arrive at the "expiration date" of our emotional wound and feel the need to transcend our pain and allow our true voice to emerge, several variables usually show up as triggers in pushing us to seek help. Psychological fatigue, discomfort, stress, lack of meaning, sadness, or disappointment can be catalysts that make us want to change or end the wound that has pursued us for so long. It is likely that a person arrives in therapy without knowing what their original wound is, but their discomfort is such that they know they have to seek help.

## The Signs

The unconscious manifests itself in several ways in order to reveal what is happening in our inner world. (By "the unconscious," I mean an aspect of our psychology that leads to the emergence of subliminal actions that impact our way of being.)

In *The Interpretation of Dreams,* Sigmund Freud wrote that the unconscious holds the key to the true motives for our behaviors and that these are unknown to us because we have repressed them. This information, which is hidden in our psyche, appears to us in the following ways:

- **Dreams** – wish fulfillment, images we perceive during the day, and unresolved aspects that are dreamed
- **Freudian slip (Parapraxis)** – involuntary errors, forgetfulness, or mistakes, slips
- **Jokes** – manifestations of the unconscious at a social level, where a feeling that cannot be directly expressed appears disguised
- **Symptoms** – a psychic imbalance between an unconscious desire and the impossibility of satisfying it, which promotes anxiety or discomfort.

These are signs that indicate we have not resolved those things that hurt us and need to pay attention. If we do not notice them, the intensity with which they manifest will increase.

Susana was very careless in various aspects of her life. Her drawers were disorganized, she arrived late to appointments, forgot to eat, and dirty dishes piled up day by day in her kitchen sink. Suddenly, she began to have a recurring dream in which giant spots appeared everywhere, everything she touched became stained, and the floor dirtied with her every footstep. Each new dream presented her with more dirt, obviously preventing her from clearly seeing what was in front of her. In her daily life, she bumped into open drawers, tripped over objects left on the floor, and had less space in her bed, as she placed dirty clothes on it. Her husband moved out because he could not cope with the chaos. At some point, Susana began to suffer from psoriasis, a chronic inflammatory skin disease that produces scaly lesions. That's when she came to therapy.

I discovered the meaning that neglect and dirt had for her, and she recalled a time in her childhood when her family was poor. Her mother had to go to work each day, as Susana's father had abandoned them when she was seven years old. Her mother became so depressed that she left her job and locked herself in her room all day.

After a long therapeutic process, Susana discovered that the disorder in her home was a way of punishing herself and confirming her belief that she did not deserve a dignified and stable life.

We worked together to bring order to her life by including specific schedules for certain activities, making calendars, and putting reminders on Post-its around her house, which contained the emotional and spiritual significance of why it was important to organize her life. Some examples of the messages on the reminders were:

- "When I order my house, I order my soul"
- "Love is in every space"
- "I am the owner of my life"
- "I deserve to enjoy my present"
- "Cleanliness is in my heart"
- "The chaos of the past is left behind."

When I was 23 years old, I broke off an engagement to a guy with whom I had a co-dependent relationship that deeply affected my self-esteem. He would often lie to me, was unfaithful, made me doubt my judgment by telling me I was exaggerating, and also criticized my body. On one occasion, we went to a bar. I went to the bathroom, and when I came out, from a distance I saw him kissing a girl. He denied it, just as he hid that he brought women back to his house after taking me home.

On the night of our engagement, he arrived an hour late. While my father toasted us and gave his speech, his hand trembled. My intuition told me everything was wrong. Suddenly I thought, *When I go on my honeymoon, I'll need to bring money to return to Mexico*, and then an image of my future appeared: I was in a dark room, taking my life. The next day, I called him to say I would not marry him.

"Why? I did not cheat on you this time," he responded.

The real reason I went into therapy was the shock I felt when I realized the self-destructive capacity with which I made decisions in my life. "They have sucked my soul," was the phrase I told the therapist. I was silent for the rest of the session.

There are transcendent moments in our lives, such as marriage, the birth of a child, the death of a loved one, losing a job, moving, divorcing, and even an unexpected professional success that destabilize us and put us in crisis. In some cases, we seek to understand what happened to us and look for the emotional tools that help us move forward.

## What Makes One Person Seek Help While Another Does Not?

After working with patients for 30 years, the impulse that brings them to my office remains a mystery. As I mentioned earlier, there are vital events and crises that motivate people to seek professional help, but not everyone struggling with a difficult path is able or willing to get help. As I said at the beginning of this book, we still don't know what it is that leads siblings to assimilate a family experience differently; the same goes for understanding the real motivation behind why people decide to attend or not attend therapy.

A single life event may be enough to prompt some people to seek help, or it may be a combination of many elements. In my experience, it is the person's spirit that brings their body to sit on a chair in my office. In psychological terms, this would be what is referred to as "temperament," the character with which we face and react to the world; that is, the personal energy we bring with us from the day we are born.

But I am also sure that a combination of factors promotes the search for awareness:

- personality traits
- familial, social, or cultural support the person has
- karma (I've seen stories that I can only explain this way)
- destiny
- life mission
- fatigue

- hopelessness
- discomfort
- obligation or pressure from family members (I do not provide therapy to those who come for this reason)
- the need to be heard and find a witness who validates their pain (these patients achieve great therapeutic results)
- looking for a life plan, or dealing with their own insecurity.

In short, these are aspects that throughout the process will determine its outcome.

Veronica was kidnapped in her youth. After 10 years, she came to me for therapy because she suffered from depression that had kept her bedridden for months.

We worked on her fears of going out, but that therapy did not help her get up. Later, we explored some childhood memories in which she felt abandoned and burdened with the responsibility of dealing with her parents' frustration and anger.

After this deep exploration, we discovered that the traumatic experience of the kidnapping was more about her family having allowed her to be taken due to the kidnappers' threats than about being terribly mistreated in captivity. The story she told herself about who she was after that event left her devastated and without the will to live: *Only someone who is worthless is abandoned like that.*

Reconstructing her place in the world took time, but when she could accept the feelings she had denied and repressed, she found new meaning for herself and the opportunity to decide how she wanted to live her life.

Whatever the reason for a patient's visit to therapy, I accompany them in discovering the essence of the story behind the reason for their consultation, which childhood wound keeps manifesting in the present, and how they can use their abilities and particular personality to strengthen their voice and true self.

In Part Two, I will share some of the tools I have used to create a path of awareness and transformation. They have been of great use to the patients I have worked with and can also be useful to others, even if they are not in a therapeutic process. It is important to note that they work to the extent that their meaning is understood, as well as their background and the intention placed in them.

# PART TWO
# I AM NOT THE WOUND
## Tools to Remember This

# 8

# SAVING YOURSELF FROM THE SHIPWRECK

We now know that the painful events of our lives are just events that happened and do not describe who we truly are. We have healed when we stop identifying with the wound and the armor we used to protect ourselves has been weakened by the strength of our authentic voice emerging.

With this newfound awareness, we can let go of the ways we have defended ourselves and choose attitudes that lead us toward an optimal version of ourselves.

## Reaching Your Own Port

Imagine you are shipwrecked at sea and find yourself clinging to a small plank. The waves are immense and submerge you every time they crash over your head. You only have moments to catch your breath before being overwhelmed again by the wall of water. You are surviving, trying not to drown, and praying not to be swallowed by a shark.

That's how the pain of an emotional wound feels. When we suffer and don't know how to resolve what's happening to us, we are "shipwrecked" in our lives and do not know where we stand.

Therapeutic work allows the strong currents to recede so that you can reach the shore. However, you are exhausted and lie on the sand for a couple of days. That's what working on the wound feels like—there you are, washed up on the beach, unable to move, can't move, the sun has burnt your skin, thirst has cracked your lips, and to top it off a crab walks across your chest.

That's how it feels to return to the pain of the past.

When you've regained some strength, you start to look around, knowing that you will remain on that island for a while, not even sure if you will ever be able to leave. Everything you have repressed comes to light. Your only motivation is to live, and you start to move, get up, and look for food and shelter. You find coconuts and palm fragments with which you build a refuge. That's what happens when you begin to leave the wound behind.

At first, the nights of silence and solitude are terrifying; some noises sound threatening. That's how the resistance to seeing the reality of our own life feels. Without realizing it, you feel increasingly confident to face whatever comes. You've learned to fish, make a fire, and gaze with wonder at the sky. You observe your thoughts, remember your story, and give it the right meaning. Your voice is the only thing you hear. That's how it feels to reach your own port. Long ago, you stopped waiting to be saved; you've become accustomed to being the hero of your own story.

## The Opportunity

It's like watching a sunset while sipping a margarita. It's waiting for us. It wants us to take it by the hand and go on the adventure to the unknown—because the wound is an opportunity for life, the crack through which the light seeps in, allowing us to see everything. The opportunity lies in seeking tools that help us live a full life that resembles who we truly are.

Each tool that follows will include an explanation of its origin and meaning, a specific exercise for anyone to develop, and an example from a clinical case. This information will give you a broad perspective of what can be done with it and its psychological, emotional, and spiritual richness. All of them serve as reminders of who we are and also promote the discipline of honoring our own existence.

# 9

# MANTRAS

## The Power of the Word

Little is known about how language developed. It is believed to have originated half a million years ago. Some hypotheses suggest that human language first developed through vocalization and gestures. It possibly appeared to indicate where food was or to protect against danger. The interaction of culture, biological evolution, and individual learning surely promoted its development.

In her book *Desnudando a la musa: ¿qué hay detrás del talento literario?* Ethel Krauze refers to Chilean biologist, philosopher, and writer Humberto Maturana (1928–2021), who trained at Harvard University in 1958 and studied language and its evolution from the field of biology, specializing in cognitive sciences. Krauze writes:

> "Maturana explains that language is capable of creating new realities by enabling increasingly subtle distinctions to be observed and described. Creativity is the generation of distinctions through recurring interactions, whose results are the emergence of new couplings, which in turn create new distinctions. That is, creativity is the most necessary characteristic in living systems. I believe this essential evolutionary skill cannot be excluded from the field of literature. All individuals, to a greater or lesser extent, have the capacity to establish recurring interactions with words and thus discover their literary creativity."

Later, I will explain how mantras can create new realities in our lives using the power of language, as mentioned by Maturana and Krauze, as well as the role creativity plays in the selection of words and the effect of their repeated pronunciation.

In their book *The Tree of Knowledge: The Biological Roots of Human Understanding*, Humberto Maturana and Francisco Varela point out that when two or more organisms interact recurrently, they produce a social coupling that allows them to improve their chances of survival. These behaviors are the first form of communication: This repeated interaction, the basis of our evolution, also occurs in the teaching–learning process.

In Krauze's words:

> "Language is a key that radically modifies human behavior and makes possible the emergence of new phenomena, such as reflection and consciousness. The distinctive feature of this key is that language enables those who operate with it to describe themselves and their circumstances through new linguistic distinctions derived from existing linguistic distinctions."

I agree with the authors that the stories we tell ourselves and the language we use to describe who we are in this world influence the choices we make in various circumstances. In Judaism, the word constitutes the expression of the soul. The identity of a person is characterized by the soul that inhabits the body, and the word is used to create tangible realities, to connect, and has the ultimate purpose of blessing others and the world around us. This is a profound and interesting philosophy because it emphasizes the sacred aspect of expression and our responsibility in using it.

Judaism also explains that when we use words to hurt, criticize, or shame, we are killing part of the person's soul. Causing shame is considered a type of murder because, when it happens, the soul wants to leave the body, creating a physiological reaction where the blood rushes to the face, which is where the soul tries to exit, and subsequently, the face turns pale for an instant when this portion of death has occurred.

This phenomenon is clearly described in the *Talmud*, a sacred book written between the 3rd and 5th centuries by Hebrew scholars. It includes rabbinic observations on Jewish laws, traditions, and customs, including Rabbi Ovadiah Bartenura, who states in *Pirkei Avot (Chapters of the Fathers)* 3:11:

> "The passage from red to white in the face shows the process in which a person responds to humiliation marked by anger and their active attempt to remove feelings of smallness. Then, the pale face (in

Hebrew, *lebanat apanim*) is marked by the shame of having been a victim. This 'mini death' occurs when the person feels paralyzed and vulnerable due to exposure and impotence."[2]

"Killing a person physically means they no longer have existence; shaming a person is driving them to feel that they no longer want to exist because of the image created of them," comments Rabbi Kanner during his current classes on religion in Mexico City.

Rabbi Samson Raphael Hirsch, a translator and German religious leader who founded the Torah im Derech School, shares this perspective:

> "Once wounded, saddened, and robbed of peace, a human being becomes sick and withers like a wilted flower. We must sacredly care for the inner sanctuary of a person and consider it as God-given soil in which we can plant our most beautiful blessings, love, and generosity. For this purpose, we have been given the noblest of gifts: the Word."[3]

*El Eco* is a documentary film directed by Tatiana Huezo and produced by Maya Scherr-Willson that won Best Documentary at the 2023 Berlinale, the Berlin International Film Festival.[4] Huezo, who is from El Salvador but lives in Mexico, explains: "This story talks about the echo that parents leave in their children, that voice that clings to the soul during the formative years and remains forever. Children learn to understand death, illness, and love with each act, word, and silence of their parents."

The documentary was filmed in the rural community of El Eco, Puebla, in a remote and solitary valley in Mexico, with a hundred inhabitants who relate to the processes of life until death in sync with their connection to the land. Similarly, their expressions and words reflect the peasant world they inhabit.

---

[2] Rabbi Aharon David Shlezinger, *Pirkei Avot Explicado: Con los comentarios de Rashi y Rabí Ovadia de Bartenura* (Spanish edition, independently published, 2021).

[3] Klugman, Rabbi Eliyahu Meir. *Rabbi Samson Raphael Hirsch. Architect of Judaism for the Modern World* (Artscroll Mesorah, 1996).

[4] Tatiana Huezo, *El Eco* (Chulada Films/Radiola Films, Mexico, 2023).

Huezo asked one of the grandmothers why the town is called El Eco. She said: "When the wind blows, it carries people's voices over the hills, and everyone can hear. That's why in this town you have to be careful with what you say."

The different perspectives I have shared regarding language and words give us an idea of the importance that the way we express ourselves has in our lives, the power of what we say in assimilating experiences, and the opportunities offered by the conscious use of words. It is for this reason that mantras are a useful tool for achieving these purposes.

## The Mantra as an Instrument

The word "mantra" comes from Sanskrit and means "liberation of the mind" (*man*: mind, *tra*: liberation). It also means "thought" or "mental instrument." Its purpose is to relax or induce a person into a meditative state and acquire spiritual or psychological power while repeating, chanting, expressing, or listening to it. Its origin is found in the *Rigveda*, a sacred text of Hinduism.

In religions such as Hinduism or Buddhism, the mantra is used as a way to support meditation or to invoke divinity through a sacred phrase, word, or syllable. Each mantra is related to a quality or aspect of personal enlightenment.

In *Definition of Mantra*, Pérez Porto and Merino explain that to evoke compassion in Buddhism, the mantra *Om mani padme hum* ("The jewel in the lotus") is used. The syllables of this mantra relate to bliss or meditation (*om*), patience (*ma*), discipline (*ni*), wisdom (*pad*), generosity (*me*), and diligence (*hum*). This is such a complete mantra that anyone seeking any of these qualities or all of them can use it, as long as they think of its meaning while reciting it.[5]

There are different types of mantras, according to the aspects a person seeks. Each has a syllabic translation that corresponds to the

---

[5] J. Pérez Porto & M. Merino, "Definition of Mantra: What It Is, Significance and Concept, and Definition" ("Definición de mantra: Qué es, Significado y Concepto, Definicion."), 27 October 2010, last modified September 27, 2022, https://definicion.de/mantra/

aspects intended to be invoked: from collective peace (*Om Sarveshaam Svastir, Bhavatu*) to pain mitigation (*Tayata Om Bekanze*) to prosperity (*Om Vasudhare Svaha*) to obtaining love (*Lokah Samastah Sukhino Bhavantu*).[6]

Some prayers can also be considered mantras. In the Christian religion, for example, rosaries are a chain of counted mantras that generate a meditative state of spiritual connection.

Psychologically and emotionally, mantras are a tool through which we can focus on an action or task, protect ourselves from situations that cause us anxiety, remind ourselves of the significance of figures we consider important for our spiritual development, relax in the face of triggers caused by childhood wounds, as well as reaffirm and change behaviors, anticipate reactions to different contexts, work through grief, or plan our life.

Mantras can support us through any moment of our lives or accompany us in the goals we wish to undertake. They are effective when we understand the real meaning of what we are saying and our intention in invoking them.

The repetition of mantras aims to create harmony between the physical self and the spiritual self. We can achieve this by paying attention to each word of the mantra, expressing them consciously and feeling them in our bodies. Finally, we experience their power when we realize that the frequency of our emotions and thoughts has risen.

Mantras have the following characteristics that prove their effectiveness:

- The phrases or words are repeated rhythmically and continuously.
- They are pronounced internally or aloud, depending on the circumstances.
- They have a specific meaning for the person.
- They have a purpose.

---

[6] Aprende Institute.com retrieved March 3, 2023 https://aprende.com/blog/bienestar/meditacion/que-es-un-mantra/

- They help the mind to release thoughts.
- Their repetition generates a deep state of consciousness.
- They focus attention.
- They are a kind of guided meditation through the use of words.

## Ira Progoff's Mantra Crystals

Ira Progoff was an American psychotherapist who developed the Intensive Journal Method at Drew University, where he was director of the Institute for Research in Depth Psychology.[7] Beginning in the 1950s, he explored various psychological methods that intervene in creativity and spiritual experiences and their application in the social dimension.

Progoff was an important figure in Carl Jung's humanistic psychology and transpersonal psychology, as well as in journal writing. He compiled the works of Sigmund Freud, Alfred Adler, Jung, and Otto Rank, which formed the basis of his theories and research regarding life cycles and their relationship with creative and spiritual experiences. The result of his research was the Intensive Journal Method developed in 1966 as a comprehensive system of techniques to interrelate the contents of personal life. In 1966, he founded Dialogue House to conduct his Intensive Journal courses. He died in 1998.

I don't remember exactly how I discovered this great author, but I immediately set out to read his book.

I was so fascinated by the depth and breadth of vision with which so many aspects of one's life could be worked on using the tool of his Intensive Journal that I contacted his son Jon to find out if they were still offering his courses. We had a couple of phone calls in which he interviewed me and provided information about the process involved in Intensive Journal work.

"Why do you want to travel so far to study this methodology?" he asked. He was intrigued by my real motivation for taking a 10-hour flight.

---

[7] Ira Progoff, *At a Journal Workshop: Writing to Access the Power of the Unconscious and Evoke Creative Ability* (Penguin Publishing Group, 1992).

I responded: "The distance I have to travel to work on my personal process doesn't matter. I will always be willing to do it."

In September 2019, I took the Intensive Journal Workshop at Ashburnham Place in the city of Battle in East Sussex, England. During a week of silence and writing, along with a group of 12 people from different parts of the world, I studied and practiced the method, which consisted of three modules:

1. Life Context
2. Deep Contact
3. Life Integration

Each module is divided into four sections that emphasize a different dimension of experience with specific procedures and exercises. The Intensive Journal Method's four dimensions are:

1. **Life/Time Dimension** – significant experiences and the person's biography in order to observe one's development and create sensitivity to the rhythm of our growth.
2. **Dialogue Dimension** – dialogue of the individual with work, body, events, society, or significant people to deepen the quality of relationships we have in our lives.
3. **Symbolic Dimension** – recording dreams and images or internal dialogues with figures we consider wise to bring to consciousness and integrate our unconscious aspects.
4. **Meditative Dimension** – recording and developing the contents and images that appear in meditation to create personal mantras from this evocation.

No prior preparation is required to attend the workshop. One only needs to bring some written images or dreams to use as material for work.

When I participated, Joanne Ching, a disciple of Jung, led the group. She had practiced the methodology for decades. In the classroom, only her voice was heard, providing theoretical information and exercise instructions. Sometimes she instructed us to say our reflections aloud, so voices in different languages, such as French, German, English, or Spanish, were heard in unison as if we were reciting a collective and multicultural mantra.

The primary objective of doing this was to promote personal work in which the introspection of unconscious language (called by many, "spiritual or soul language") rose to the surface and allowed the individual to understand where things stood in their life. As Ira Progoff said at a Journal Workshop in 1975: "Each person goes through the well of his or her own life to the depth level that is beyond the well and beyond the person."

Opinions, observations, or comments were prohibited, and silence was fundamental for such immersion. In this way, the journey into the inner world developed from writing in the Intensive Journal and its various sections in a group setting. Because everyone in the group was there for the same purpose, this generated an atmosphere of energy and synchronicity and thus, the containment needed for us to navigate our individual searches.

Remaining in active listening without offering opinions promoted the dissolution of our individuality, and the collective soul surpassed the language barriers, so when a student shared a reflection in their native language, the emotion emanating from their voice made their words understandable.

For several days, we shared our echoes; worked silently on our dreams and the symbols emerging from our memories; created our personal mantras; metaphorically dialogued with people, events, and situations in our lives; and witnessed the emotional journeys of our companions, their introspections, and the sudden cries that writing led us to. During that week, I experienced revealing dreams, and as time went on, the language of my spirit became clearer. It was as if a world with a life of its own beyond waking life opened up before me.

When I returned to Mexico, I practiced creating mantras with my patients based on the meanings and desires each had for their lives. It was surprising how powerful this tool became for the flow of the therapeutic process. I made some modifications and added some different elements to Progoff's original approach, which I will discuss in the exercise section.

## Why Did Ira Progoff Call Them Mantra Crystals?

Ira Progoff called the instrument used for creative spiritual practice "mantra crystals," vehicles through which a person connects with the deepest dimensions of the psyche. The function of Mantra Crystals is to crystallize our inner reality and materialize it through consciousness. To achieve this, the individual's images and dreams are drawn from their experience. As Progoff said at a Journal Workshop in 1980, "The purpose is to have a means to focus and deepen people's consciousness in order to evaluate the meditation process in its broader aspects."

***Note: The mantras I refer to in this book are personalized ones. They can be created and used as a tool for psychological and spiritual aid in life, depending on the relevant and significant aspects the person chooses. They are not pre-established mantras like those in Buddhism or Hinduism but have similar effects.***

Progoff created Mantra Crystals by taking traditional religious mantras as a starting point and building on the concept to create an effective tool in the practice of contemporary deep holistic psychology. In so doing, he shifted from the traditional stance of introducing the use of mantras into personal life from an external source to having them emerge organically from the individual's life story. He also points out that, rather than having a mantra given to oneself as an external intrusion, it is only through experiences rooted in the total context of life that deep spiritual factors can be absorbed into individual development.

For the reasons mentioned above, when significant or crucial situations occur for the patient within the therapeutic process, I find the opportunity to create a mantra that crystallizes that experience and places it in consciousness through the selection of representative words and their repetition. Relevant situations or moments can be related to a revelation, intense emotional pain, the recognition of a childhood wound, or the conviction to generate a change in attitude.

By honoring each individual's unique life story, the methodology developed by Progoff allows their internal spiritual guide to emerge from the experiences that have been part of their life. In this way, Mantra Crystals form the links among their past experiences as the individual moves toward their future. Thus, the mantra symbolizes a small representative piece of a large and significant inner experience from their past.

Lorena was afraid to express her true thoughts and feelings to her mother regarding her perception of marriage, as her mother believed that success for women meant getting married and having children. Lorena, however, thought that success for women meant freedom and personal fulfillment through a profession.

This difference in perspective kept my patient from feeling confident enough to tell her mother about her dreams and desires, as during her childhood, she had learned that to receive her parents' love she had to engage in activities they considered feminine and that she would be reprimanded if she expressed what she really wanted and be called "rebellious." The crucial moment occurred when she was forced to go out with a boy Lorena detested but whom her parents considered "from a good family."

We spent a month exploring all the implications and meanings this event had in her life story. When she decided to confront her parents, she had spent a couple of weeks practicing and repeating the personal mantra we had constructed for her in therapy: "I am free." She had concluded that her belief in not being able to be free was much more powerful than her parents' expectations and possible rejection, so the mantra had to include elements of freedom. Thus, her personal mantra aimed to strengthen her freedom and consequently eradicate the fears related to her freedom.

After understanding, absorbing, and repeating a mantra that was loaded with meaning for her, Lorena was able to oppose her parents' wishes and successfully continue with her professional career.

The concept of Mantra Crystals is an allusion to the process whereby crystals form as a result of molten liquid cooling and coming into contact with invisible warm vapor that has been exposed to a colder surface, thus becoming a different substance.

Progoff took this concept and metaphorically applied it to psychotherapy as a means of compressing small but significant aspects of broader experiences into a new channel for future experiences. In a 1980 publication on process meditation, he noted, "Crystal is a miniature of the atmosphere of the larger whole, as well as a vehicle to focus previous experiences in a new form."[8]

Within the methodology of the Intensive Journal, Mantra Crystals provide a means of linking past experiences with new developments of meaning in a person's life. They are a kind of meditation in which the mantra tends to establish an atmosphere of personal-cosmic connection. Within this atmosphere, internal changes and experiences occur, and for this to happen, it works alongside directed breathing. The active holistic principle underlying symbolic experience in spiritual practice is that the deeply experienced symbol is the reality that develops in one's life.

In Progoff's words: "The symbol is the reality that is becoming the established condition of a person's life made real through an entire outer/inner experience."[9]

After integrating and understanding the importance of language and words and the meaning of mantras and their power in our lives, I will next share a practical exercise that can be used by anyone who wants to use this tool to prepare, connect spiritually, face situations in their life, strengthen their self-esteem, remember the reasons behind their actions, or for any other activity their creativity chooses.

---

[8] Ira Progoff, *Process Meditation* (Dialogue House Library, 1980).

[9] Ira Progoff, *Process Meditation*.

## Putting the Mantra into Practice

This exercise is based on the principles in Progoff's Intensive Journal Method, as I find his methodology comprehensive and solid. I have only made a few adjustments to simplify the eight steps in creating personal mantras:

1. **Reflect on the purpose of the mantra:** The first step in including a mantra in our lives is to reflect on its purpose. It can be something complex (helping to make the decision to get a divorce) or quite simple (remembering to smile at the doorman).
2. **Write the meaning:** Once we have chosen the topic, circumstance, personality trait, fear, or life project we want to work on, we move on to the second step, which is to write a few sentences about the meaning the topic has for us. It's important not to go overboard; an appropriate number is between six and eight sentences.
3. **Conscious pronunciation:** After writing the sentences, we move on to the third step, where we read them out loud a couple of times, paying attention to our breathing (whether it's agitated or relaxed) and to each of the words in them, pronouncing them slowly.
4. **Selection of significant words:** In the fourth step, we underline a maximum of 10 words that seem relevant or representative regarding our theme or personal history. One way to find out which words these are is to observe how they make us feel and what they mean to us. For example, for one person, "justice" may be more relevant than "equity"; for another, they may need both words in order to strengthen the meaning of their mantra.
5. **Constructing the mantra:** The fifth step involves writing the words on a separate sheet and observing them. These precise words may remind us of past experiences, be the ones we use regularly, evoke a certain emotion, or be used by someone else when addressing us. We then choose how many words we want to include in our mantra. The longer it is, the harder it will be to remember, and perhaps the strength of its meaning will diminish. This doesn't mean that you can't incorporate the 10 chosen words. However, the precision of our language and its meaning will determine the effect on our purpose. Furthermore, repetitions will help reinforce the concept we want to work on and bring to consciousness.

6. **Establish the order of the words in the phrase:** Now, in the sixth step, we decide on the order in which we will arrange the words of our mantra. It's important that they are related to each other and that together they form a concept integrated into the purpose we will carry out (in the mantra "I am free," the selected words form a total concept that is also integrated by parts that have meaning in themselves: "I am" speaks to one's own existence, identity, and everything the person considers about themselves. "Free," here the word refers to the general concept but also to the individual and specifically what it represents for the individual. "I am free" is a combination of two words that together enhance their meaning and energetic content).
7. **Integrate breathing into the mantra:** Depending on the final number of words we have chosen for our mantra; the seventh step will involve the number of inhalations and exhalations we make as we recite it. One way to guide breathing with pronunciation of the words is to divide each word into syllables and see how our inhalation and exhalation line up when pronouncing them. For example: "I am free" (inhalation) "and I believe it (exhalation). Each person will feel in their own body the best way to match their breathing with the words.
8. **Trial and error:** After constructing our mantra, the eighth step is to test it. We do this by checking how we feel when reciting it for a few days, and if it's producing the desired effects. At any point, we can change it, either because we are not comfortable with it or because our emotions and goals have changed regarding our initial purpose; or even better, we have achieved what we were looking for. The creation process can be used as many times as needed for different aspects of our lives and the events that happen to us that we want to address consciously.

## Clinical Case: To Reach the Top of a Mountain

A few years ago, I met Pablo, a young man who had attempted suicide. He was in his twenties, charismatic, intelligent, and confident when speaking. He had taken a gap year trip and upon returning to Mexico felt distant from his friends and out of place.

During our first session, Pablo told me about how he had fantasized about ending his life and described the act of attempting to do so, which luckily was not successful.

I looked at him intently and said, "I don't believe you."

Surprised, he replied that what he had told me was true and that he didn't understand what I was trying to say.

So, I completed the sentence, "It doesn't seem to me that you are someone who wants to end their life; perhaps you just don't know how to live it right now."

A couple of sessions later, he confessed that among the professionals he had interviewed I was the one he had chosen for a specific reason.

"And why is that?" I asked.

"You saw the possibility, while the others worried about and pitied me. I would have never moved forward from that point," he said.

From the start, Pablo had noticed the offer I had extended to him to focus his energy on being present in life. It was good, he thought, that this therapist saw more in him than what he was presenting outwardly at the moment.

As part of his therapeutic process, we went through various aspects of his life—from his relationship with his parents, childhood wounds, rejection by his friends, building the life he wanted, and the profession he desired to study and practice to the confident and assertive attitude he chose to have toward life.

Pablo was receptive and committed to his process, working diligently on the tasks I assigned and implementing all the tools he was learning.

He became interested in reading books on the subject of meditation and learning the different techniques I offered him, and of course, we created mantras at different times and performed rituals. He would anticipate the sessions with notes he wanted to work on in therapy and ask for practical suggestions on which tool was most appropriate to use in each situation.

Eventually, I discharged him and didn't hear from him for a couple of years until I received terrible news: He had had a serious accident in which he had fallen off a mountain while skiing and had broken bones throughout his body and sustained multiple head injuries that had left him in a coma.

On hearing this, I wrote to his mother and said, "Your son has a strong spirit and will wake up." And he did.

I offered to resume therapy with him through video conferencing, and shortly afterwards, Pablo contacted me from the hospital where he was recovering. He still needed a wheelchair to support his torso and head, but his accident had not diminished his will to work using the same discipline and commitment as he had in the past.

Pablo remained in hospital for four months, during which time his main focus was on recovering the parts of his brain that had been damaged, affecting certain memory and concentration functions. His spirit remained intact and strengthened, reflected in him making jokes about his condition and showing gratitude for being alive. Sometimes, he experienced a lot of pain after sessions with the orthopedic surgeon; other times, he felt deeply moved by the suffering of other patients.

His intellectual capacity was one of the aspects he valued most about himself, so he was keen to acquire tools to recover his short-term memory and restore the damaged neural network. He worked with his neurologists on various exercises to rebuild the neural connections in his brain, which required significant effort and frustration. Taking care of his spirit and emotions was the focus of our shared space.

Discussing all the aspects covered in our work together would be impossible, so I will specifically focus on the mantra we built to help Pablo gradually recover his intellectual functions. The construction process was similar to what I detailed in the exercise section, but I will share a brief outline.

Initially, we reviewed the functions that represented an improvement in his quality of life and a recovery of his intellectual faculties, a fundamental part of his being. This purpose guided the creation of his personal mantra.

I want to mention that this process was initiated by Pablo, who told me, "I remember the mantras we created in the past, and I want a new one to help me move forward from this situation." He then wrote meaningful sentences related to recovering his quality of life and intellectual faculties. Some of them were:

◊ Being **present** in the moment, developing absolute **awareness** and attention.
◊ Having the ability to enjoy life.
◊ Setting a goal and achieving it. Knowing that I am capable of facing whatever comes.
◊ Knowing how to let go.
◊ Understanding what I can control and what I can't. Aligning my **thoughts** and **actions**.
◊ Utilizing my **energy** to understand what's happening.
◊ Using my **intuition**.

After reading the sentences aloud and analyzing them, Pablo highlighted the words he found significant: present, attitude, thought, action, energy, and intuition. He wrote a number representing the order of appearance of each word in the sentence. He also chose to add some verbs denoting actions for each word:

◊ Present
◊ Awareness
◊ Intuition
◊ Energy
◊ Thought
◊ Action

Finally, he crafted his personal mantra:

"I live in the present with awareness, focusing my intuition and energy, creating synergy between my thought and action."

After practicing his breathing and observing his body, he decided on a three-step breathing pattern:

(inhalation) – "I live in the present with awareness"
(exhalation) – "focusing my intuition and energy"
(inhalation) – "creating synergy between my thought and action"

This is followed by exhalation, then inhalation to begin the phrase again.

This mantra accompanied him throughout his recovery for several more months. I discharged him once more. Recently, he sent me a photograph of himself at the summit of Iztaccíhuatl, with a note that read, "I was a survivor, now I live in the present."

10

# RITUALS

## The Emotional Ceremony

Ceremonies and rituals have existed since humans have inhabited this planet. Surely, at the beginning of time, people engaged in these practices, organically and spontaneously, to understand their surroundings and perhaps to combat the uncertainty of their own existence.

A ritual is essentially a set of ceremonial actions that have symbolic or representative value; they can be inscribed in an ideology, a creed, a cultural tradition, or a social custom. A ritual's main purpose is to reinforce a bond in any area sought, whether to unite people toward a common purpose of spirituality, a social or political objective, or a mystical practice. The regularity with which it is performed increases its strength.

It is fascinating to delve into the history of rituals and ceremonial aspects of cultures and remote eras, as well as to understand the different approaches to studying the subject. I will share only a few approaches with the intention of offering basic information that will later support ways in which we can work rituals into our lives.

Ceremonies and rituals are like sketches that contain worldviews, cultural expressions, and symbolic relationships with the world. As such, I will now explore the philosophical, anthropological, literary, and Jungian and systemic psychology perspectives of contemplating the vast landscape of rituals.

## Philosophical Vision

At the end of the AD 200s and beginning of the AD 300s, the term "theurgy" appeared in the Chaldean oracles, a collection of hexameters (the composition and structure of epic verse in ancient Greek and Latin poetry) revealed by the gods. Their content was theological and technical and related to ritual instructions that for philosophers represented texts of metaphysical and poetic wisdom. These oracles, which were sacred books, disappeared during the burning of the Great Library of Alexandria, and only some fragments remain.

According to the Chaldean oracles, theurgy is the specific practice of the Hellenic mystical tradition and is related to the wisdom of the Chaldeans that combined literary tradition and ritual technique.

Followers of Plato used the term theurgy to refer to the art of communicating and collaborating with the gods through this ritual technique, which includes any mystical, religious, and magical practice, and serves as a philosophical metaphor that seeks the unification of the soul with the Divine. This combination of the philosophical approach to divinity and ritual techniques offered a vision of humans as spiritual beings on an inner quest through philosophy that allows them to know the world.

Writer George Robert Stow Mead was a member of the Theosophical Society, an international fraternity dedicated to theosophy (the knowledge and learning of reality through the comparative study of religion, science, and philosophy, to discover the fundamental teaching of each). In his book *The Chaldean Oracles: Fragments of the Alexandrian Gnosis*, Mead offers various comments on the text that is preserved from the Alexandrian Gnosis, which was part of Hellenic philosophy.

## Anthropological Vision

In the anthropological vision, rituals have been fundamental in the study of human evolution, society's idiosyncrasies, and cultural aspects.

In his 1970 book *The Forest of Symbols: Aspects of Ndembu Ritual*, Victor Turner, a Scottish cultural anthropologist who studied the rites and symbols of tribal cultures and their impact on societies, presents a series of anthropological studies of African society. He provides a detailed record of the semantics of the symbols that make up the rituals, combining an ethnographic description based on fieldwork among the Ndembu of Zambia and his theoretical contribution. Furthermore, he describes ritual practices and their psychological and sociological implications within a preliterate society. He also includes case studies illustrating how ritual unifies and harmonizes the community, giving it some stability. Additionally, he documents data on rituals such as circumcision.

For Turner, symbols are forces that act in social processes and fulfill certain functions in ceremonies and rituals. In "Social Dramas and Stories about Them" in *Critical Inquiry* (1980), he defines a ritual symbol as "the smallest unit of ritual that still retains the specific properties of ritual behavior." The symbol "is something that, by general consensus, is thought to naturally typify, represent, or recall something, whether through possession of analogous qualities or by association of fact or thought. The symbols I observed in the field were empirically objects, activities, relationships, events, gestures, and spatial units in a ritual context."

Later on, I will explain the concept of including symbolic elements in rituals that represent the idiosyncrasies and inner world we want to manifest.

Émile Durkheim was a French sociologist and anthropologist who ventured into modern sociology. His view was that society shapes individuals in its image through religious, political, and moral beliefs that control them.

For Durkheim, ritual is a mechanism that produces society's integration and reproduces its basic structures to reinforce its roles and status. The aim of this social integration function is to compel members of the group to share a set of collective beliefs and thus, be represented and expressed and able to maintain their unity. For Victor Turner, however, ritual also represents conflicts so that, through this representation (ritual) they are recognized and integrated.

Roy Rappaport, an American anthropologist, conducted ritual studies. In his book *Pigs for the Ancestors: Ritual in the Ecology of a New Guinea People*, he describes a classic case study of the ecology of the Maring Tsembaga tribal society, and the roles of culture and ritual in preserving society.

In his text, Rappaport shows his functional vision of cultures where the population relates to its natural environment to satisfy its biological needs. The Maring, for example, had a ritual of pig sacrifice during times of war, conducted by tribe members to absolve their debts through the use of supernatural forces. They fattened the pigs and then sacrificed them as offerings to the ancestors to provide food for the tribe, prevent land degradation, and moderate wars.

In my private practice, I have had the opportunity to observe how social, cultural, and religious contexts influence patients' beliefs and perspectives on how to have an ideal life that corresponds to collective demands and expectations. When the collective negatively affects their individual expression, I use the various tools described in this book to balance this duality and strengthen their voice within their environment.

In my methodology, I propose creating individual rituals as an important function to extract relevant meanings from the patient's life and represent them in an action.

## Literary Vision

Byung-Chul Han, a South Korean philosopher, is currently a professor at the University of the Arts in Berlin specializing in cultural studies and one of the most widely read scholars today.

In his book *The Disappearance of Rituals*, he emphasizes how rituals have lost their strength in the present day due to, among other things, digital communication, which leads to the loss of community that needs interpersonal relationships to sustain its foundation.

The immediacy of current communication makes rituals unnecessary and, therefore, obsolete, causing people to require less and less ceremonialism to create bonds.

Han believes that symbolic forms unify society and that when they are no longer cultivated, the community deteriorates and people become disoriented. He also mentions that rituals are symbolic actions that serve to recognize the world and give it permanence. Their repetition allows a deeper understanding of an aspect than the first time it is experienced.

Rituals are so powerful that several writers have used them to write their texts, build their characters, and develop the plots of their stories. Based on various sources and interviews, here are some examples:

- Juan Rulfo, a Mexican writer, wrote his novel *Pedro Páramo* on little papers of different colors that contained the situations occurring in the novel. The colors represented the hierarchy and importance within the story, and after arranging the hierarchies, he would rewrite the text.
- Gabriel García Márquez, winner of the Nobel Prize in Literature in 1982, would wake up at 5 a.m., read for two hours, bathe, and have breakfast. Then he would review the manuscript from the previous day and start writing, dressed but barefoot (he never wrote in pajamas). He always had to have a yellow flower on the table. He did not keep notes of his ideas; he simply kept them in his mind and later developed them in his works. To test his stories, he would tell them at a conference to see how people reacted, then write the opposite of what he had said.
- Isabel Allende, a Chilean writer, and author of such books as *The House of the Spirits*, *A Long Petal of the Sea*, *The Soul of a Woman*, and *Violeta*, includes mysticism and spirituality and magical realism in her writing. When she starts writing, she lights a candle, and if it goes out, she stops writing for the day. She also performs spells and uses fetishes. She always starts writing her books on January 8th.

## Jungian Psychological Vision

To talk about rituals from a psychological perspective, I have chosen to share one of my favorite authors due to his unparalleled research and studies on the collective unconscious, archetypes, mythology, symbols, anthropology, alchemy, dream interpretation, synchronicity, art, comparative religion, and philosophy: Carl Gustav Jung.

C.G. Jung was a Swiss psychiatrist, psychologist, and essayist. He is considered a key figure in psychoanalysis alongside Sigmund Freud and later founded the Analytic or Depth Psychology School.

I recall that after graduating with a degree in clinical psychology, I was faced with the dilemma of what type of therapeutic approach I wanted to specialize in. By then, it was clear to me that reductionist theories and behavior modification did not resonate with my personality and life perspective, so I opted to investigate the Latin American

Institutes of Family Studies A.C. (ILEF) and the Mexican Institute of the Couple (AMETEP).

My vision was focused on achieving effective work with people by getting to the root of what had emotionally troubled them. Thus, I decided to pursue a master's and doctorate at AMETEP, as it had a Jungian-oriented study program (which I did not fully know but found solid).

Indeed, the basis of my professional and therapeutic practice has been the result of that training period, as working with the language of the soul (symbols, dreams, myths, rituals, mantras, and creative processes) has been how I discovered that childhood wounds can be truly and deeply healed.

It is worth mentioning that as part of my working philosophy, I have never given a clinical diagnosis to a patient, and surprisingly, none have ever asked for one. The reason for this decision stems from my certainty that a human being is much more than their emotional illness or mental disorders. Their being is not fragmented but composed of various parts—body, mind, and soul—which reside within the wholeness of their spirit. In this completeness lie all possibilities for healing.

I have discovered that many variables fall outside our control when transmitting a diagnosis and how it is received. This does not mean that I do not have a diagnosis of the patient, but instead of pigeonholing them into clinical nomenclature, I review the patient's life situations with them, and how they have faced or avoided them, to develop the particular tools that will help them achieve the life they want and are willing to have.

Instead of using terminology that in many cases scares, paralyzes, or demotivates a patient, I focus on describing how they experience life circumstances and the qualities of their personality that help them face them, as well as the aspects of themselves they need to pay attention to that lead them into conflict or poor decision-making.

Some colleagues have questioned my stance, because they believe that giving a diagnosis is useful; but not giving it is also valid, as long as the patient's symptoms are addressed with seriousness and professional dedication.

Perhaps there should be ethical standards for giving a diagnosis. Here are some that come to mind:

- The professional must know the patient as broadly as possible in order to establish their diagnosis.
- There must be a solid, empathetic, and trusting therapeutic relationship.
- The therapist has explored various alternatives and tools with the patient to improve their life.
- The therapist considers the patient in their entirety and does not define their spirit by their childhood wound or mental disorder.
- The therapist trusts their patient's ability and capacity to heal.
- The patient must be ready to receive the information the therapist wants to convey. The therapist must be aware of the opportune moment to provide the information.
- The therapist must choose their words carefully and consider the impact they will have when conveyed.
- The therapist may give a diagnosis to the patient if they are receptive to receiving it.
- The therapist must take care of the patient's self-esteem and offer alternatives and an action plan as part of the therapeutic accompaniment.
- If the patient expressly requests their diagnosis, consider providing emotional tools to help them assimilate the information.

But let's go back to the greatest of the greats: Jung.

Here are some basic ideas from the 2009 edition of Jung's *The Red Book*. He wrote the book in 1913, after suffering a psychological crisis resulting from a hallucination in which he saw Europe in the midst of a catastrophe. This experience made him question whether these visions were triggered by some external war circumstance or if it was his unconscious.

## Images and Archetypes

Jung decided to work on and pay attention to the psychic content that arose by translating his emotions into images (for example, the emotion of anger can be correlated with the symbol of an erupting volcano). He describes his process as follows: "My experiment affirmed to me the therapeutic value of making conscious the images that lie behind the emotions."

As part of his methodology, Jung noted all his fantasies in The Red Book and developed the symbolic content, together with the accompanying emotions. The images appeared spontaneously, emanating from the unconscious, without his intention to construct or plan them. He observed that the images could be related to painful psychic experiences. Sometimes I propose this strategy to open the possibility of healing the wound.

For example, starting from these symbolic images—the erupting volcano, the flowing river, the sound of birds—we can explore their meanings. The same symbol can represent various aspects for a person, depending on their experiences and perceptions. The symbol is, therefore, an image with energy that impacts the emotional realm, and vice versa.

These experiences crystallize and condense in the symbolic images, which are the memory of those experiences. From a broader perspective, archetypes are emotional and behavioral patterns that come from the collective unconscious and determine our perception of reality, images, and the world.

According to Jung, the symbol is "the expression of something that cannot be characterized better. The symbol is alive as long as it remains pregnant with meaning"; that is, symbols help us uncover psychic contents in the form of images or representations that we can understand without needing to describe them in words.

In his book *The Archetypes and the Collective Unconscious*, Jung noted that archetypes form the structure of the soul and are the bridge that connects the earth with the sky; that is, the earthly world with fantasy. According to my observations, the archetypes that have a far-reaching impact consist of representations inherited from our ancestors that repeat over time and across the planet identically (for example, the content of legends is similar in many places). The symbol, in turn, allows the invisible to be made visible through the implementation of the ritual.

## Mandalas

Mandalas were another tool that Jung used to reach the unconscious because they are symbols captured in complex drawings, generally circular and concentric, representing the forces that balance the universe. The word *mandala* comes from Sanskrit and means "circle or disk." In Eastern philosophies, they are used as meditation tools and have a creative purpose of expression.

For Jung, the Tibetan mandala is a contemplation tool whereby the circular narrowing of the visual field toward the center produces self-concentration in the meditator. He considers its basic colors to be red, green, white, and yellow, "since they represent the four cardinal points and, at the same time, psychic functions" that express individuation (the process of becoming an autonomous individual with a unique identity). He also refers to the different circles that form the mandala as "magic circles" that help produce "the passage of unconscious contents to consciousness in patients or psychoanalyzed people."

He considers the mandala a symbol as it represents a reality conveyed through pencil, brush, and paper but hides another that is not manifested, not fully known, and discovered as one concentrates on the drawing. It is a symbol that shows the principles of the world, such as the union of opposites contained within Yin and Yang and Heaven and Earth.

These are symbols that have appeared throughout time, place, and cultures, so there is a collective unconscious beyond the individual. In *The Red Book*, Jung states:

> "I could show many more pictures from different parts of the world, and it would be surprising to see that these symbols obey the same basic laws observed in individual mandalas . . . one is forced to record that beyond the conscious must be an unconscious disposition for the individual and of universal extension, so to

> speak, a disposition that, in principle, can produce the same symbols at any time and place, or at least very similar symbols.
>
> Since this disposition is usually unconscious for the individual, I have named it the collective unconscious and posited primordial images, the archetypes, as the basis of its symbolic products. The identity of individual unconscious contents with their ethnic parallels is not only expressed in figurative form but also in meaning."

On the other hand, Jung attributes to the mandala the representation of the divine image in the soul; that is, where human and divine essence converge and are integrated as a totality encompassing the conscious and unconscious aspects of the person. The image of divinity can be observed in the symbols characterizing the world, nature, and man.

Jung applied his own method of active imagination, a technique through which one can observe and analyze unconscious contents, including writing the narration of his fantasies, which he then drew in the form of mandalas.

In *Memories, Dreams, and Reflections*, he says: "In the symbols, the union of conscious and unconscious contents is realized. From this union derive new situations or positions of consciousness: the transcendent function. Making the personality a totality is the goal of psychotherapy that does not merely aim to cure symptoms."

*Goddesses in Every Woman* is a book by the American author Jean Shinoda Bolen, a psychiatrist, writer, and Jungian analyst. In it, Shinoda Bolen develops a new psychology of the female gender by presenting archetypes and comparing them with Greek goddesses and their general traits. In her text, she explains that when a woman understands her own internal patterns, she can overcome dilemmas and conflicts. She describes these patterns through the form of seven archetypal goddesses representing different types of personalities and traits:

- Artemis – autonomous
- Athena – cold and calculating
- Demeter – nurturing

- Aphrodite – creative
- Hera – violent and vengeful
- Persephone – innocent
- Hestia – patient.

The symbolic contents of the archetypes are transmitted across multiple generations and include concepts like love, fear, or the notion of depth.

In an experiment aimed at proving the innate existence of archetypes, a one-year-old baby was encouraged to crawl over a flat surface that was half concrete and half transparent acrylic. The child crawled to the edge of the concrete and stopped at the surface that appeared to have depth. This exercise demonstrated that the information about depth was already integrated into the baby, even though no one had taught it; they simply knew they would fall into that "precipice" if they advanced.

Another interesting archetypal example is what happens in the Sacred Monkey Forest Sanctuary in Ubud, Bali. This is a Hindu temple in the middle of a forest where monkeys live freely.

The temple construction is based on the Hindu teaching to maintain a harmonious relationship to life: *Tri Hita Karana*, or "Three Ways to Happiness" (*Tri* = "three," *Hita* = "happiness," and *Karana* = "form"). These include:

1. Among human beings
2. Among humans and their environment
3. Among humans and the Supreme God.

Besides being a sacred sanctuary for monkeys, this temple is used to research the social interactions of monkeys, both with each other and their environment. One discovery scientists have made is that monkeys react violently when humans bare their teeth. This has led to the conclusion that showing the teeth symbolizes aggression and triggers defensive behavior in monkeys.

In my view, this archetype of aggression may have been transmitted from generation to generation with the monkeys' response now instinctive, but perhaps it results from a form of collective wisdom that has been unconsciously passed down. According to Jung, psychic energy is something that is both potentiated and timeless.

## Systemic Psychological Vision

In 1974, ritual was included within systemic family therapy models by Mara Selvini Palazzoli, founder of the Milan School. This therapeutic model is described as "an action or series of actions, accompanied by verbal formulas and involving the entire family. Like any ritual, it must consist of a regular sequence of steps taken at the appropriate time and in the right place."

Palazzoli's book *Self-Starvation: From the Intrapsychic to the Transpersonal Approach to Anorexia Nervosa* includes brief examples of clinical cases where family rituals were employed.

One representative case reported by the Milan School after the book's publication involved a burial ritual for a family with a young daughter who had stopped eating after the death of her younger brother, four days after he was born. (It's worth mentioning that nobody had explained to the little girl what had happened.) In this ritual, the parents told their daughter about the death of the baby so that she could understand it, and together, they took the baby's clothes and buried them while talking about his death. After this experience, the girl "digested" her brother's death and started eating again.

Milan group therapists emphasized the effectiveness of these rituals, saying: "Family rituals of this type are among the most important and effective therapeutic techniques we have conceived in our research to achieve rapid and decisive intervention with dysfunctional families."[10]

---

[10] Mara Selvini Palazzoli, *Self-Starvation: From the Intrapsychic to the Transpersonal Approach to Anorexia Nerviosa* (Human Context Books, 1974).

## Therapeutic Rituals: My Methodology

Rituals help us process certain emotions through the use of symbols; that is, rituals work alongside the therapeutic process to achieve balance between the patient's emotions and their images or symbols. Specifically, they are tasks the person puts into action and are linked to psychic content.

Another important purpose of therapeutic rituals is that they help the patient transition through different moments in their life, prepare for the beginning or closure of certain situations, or give new meaning to their life experiences.

Optimal execution of a therapeutic ritual occurs when the relationship between the therapist and the patient is solid, as crafting it requires a certain level of trust and conviction for the involved psychic content to come to life. I believe that disposition and attitude are probably important elements, too, especially since the goal is to make the invisible visible as a form of invocation.

For those of us passionate about tennis, it is hard to ignore the ritual of recurring gestures and actions that tennis player Rafael Nadal, winner of 22 Grand Slam titles, performed before and during matches: He pulled up his socks to the same height, lined up his water bottles perfectly, brushed the court line with his foot, and avoided stepping on lines after finishing a game. He had a specific order for wiping sweat off his brow, passing his wrists over his face, touching his ears, and pulling his shorts from the back.

Nadal stated:

> "These are silly things we players do over the years. We play many matches during the season, feel pressure, and seek routines that make us feel more comfortable. These rituals help me feel totally focused on the goal. When I train, I have no rituals, but when I'm competing, they give me security and isolation from distracting factors."

It is interesting that Nadal mentioned the concepts of focus, security, and isolation, as they coincide with some characteristics of therapeutic rituals, such as:

- Paying attention to something specific (focus)
- Associating the image with the emotion that strengthens the action (security)
- Reflecting and abstracting from the act itself (isolation).

Similarly, Serbian tennis player Novak Djokovic, who has won 24 Grand Slam titles, the most in history, has a ritual of eating grass at Wimbledon after winning each title there, saying, "The taste of the grass is very good here."

One ritual I find interesting is the one that bullfighters perform when dressing before entering the arena. Each bullfighter has a particular ritual. Each has a *mozo* (an assistant) who helps them put on the bullfighting suit. The suits are hand-made, with black velvet sleeves, a tight belt, a short jacket with pronounced shoulder pads, decorative buttons, and reflective sequins, hence the name *traje de luces* ("suit of lights"). The *manoletinas* (slippers) must be placed in a particular way on the ground, while the *mozo* places the *taleguilla* (special suit pants). These are tied below the knees with strings ending in tassels and have a waistband that reaches the chest and is adjusted with buttons or clasps and held up by suspenders. The sides of the pants are embroidered with gold and silver, and an internal corset compresses, stylizes, and protects the bullfighter. Finally, he puts on the *manoletinas* and the *castañeta* (the pigtail that goes on the hair).

This ritual is conducted in complete silence until the bullfighter indicates readiness to enter the ring. They usually entrust themselves to saints or different Virgin Mary images, with devotion in prayer being one of the most crucial elements for their perceived success or failure. They typically pray in the chapel at the bull ring.

The ways the bullfighter perform his tasks, the number of rounds he takes around the bull ring, and his victorious exit atop the shoulders of others start with him picking up up a handful of sand. All of his gestures, attitudes, words, and exclamations are filled with meaning and reflect emotions that occur inside the bull ring and impact the spectators: hope, disappointment, joy, and sadness; the triumph of life over death embodied in the bull; and the ritual marks on the bull's body.

This is not merely a spectacle but an essential part of the ritual, which along with the collective reactions of the crowd and shouts of *ole!*, define the emotions derived from the bullfighter's performance and the work of art just completed.

## Functions of Rituals

In the therapeutic realm, I propose that ritual should have the following 12 functions:

1. Manifest the emotions involved in certain experiences of the person, of which they are already aware, such as being impulsive and wanting to change.
2. Support the patient through different moments in their life with a specific purpose, such as ending a relationship.
3. Serve as a reminder of the objective, or the "why," behind certain actions, such as letting go of grief.
4. Act as a bridge between symbolic content and its corresponding action, such as lighting a candle to represent the illumination of the path.
5. Align with the person's unique attitudes, such as how they show love and express it in words or actions.
6. Provide a different or broader meaning to thoughts, emotions, and actions, such as the strength to set boundaries and achieve goals.
7. Assist in planning and anticipation of the ritual as the elements come together, such as the inclusion of elements like candles, and so on.
8. Promote introspection and reflection as a result of the choice of elements used in the ritual; that is, give meaning to every aspect, such as "the candle to illuminate my path."
9. Facilitate emotional release, such as "I release the responsibility that was assigned to me."

10. Contextualize the affirmations the person must remember before a situation; that is, the use of mantras, as explained above.
11. Lead to material changes, internally and externally, as a result of the person participating in the ritual; that is, they make better decisions after the ritual.
12. Promote the installation of new psychic perspectives through the sequence and repetition used in the ritual, such as changing attitude.

As observed in psychotherapy, ritual is not just a set of previously planned and structured symbolic acts and interactions, along with their execution; it also considers the entire preparation process, what the patient experiences when performing it, and the significance of ritual renewal in their life.

## Creating of Rituals

This exercise is based on principles presented in Jung's *Red Book*. As I did with mantras, I have made some adjustments to facilitate the creation and execution of rituals.

The following eight steps include the search for the symbol that represents the emotion or circumstance that one wants to work on, the way of deciphering the energy contained in that symbol, and the archetypal trait that the patient is manifesting:

1. **Choose the emotion, conflict, or situation:** As I mentioned previously, a good time to consider performing a personal ritual is by paying attention to what causes us intense emotion, fear, unease, if we feel blocked by a situation, or simply if we want to reinforce a specific behavior attitude.
2. **Choose the main symbol:** An analogy is made between the emotion we experience and the image that can represent it ("I feel my anger is like a volcano erupting"). In this case, anger is the emotion, and the erupting volcano is the symbol.

3. **Choose a secondary symbol:** This symbol is opposite to the main one and counteracts or complements it and also carries an emotion ("I feel tranquility beside a flowing river"). In this case, tranquility is the emotion, and flowing river water is the symbol.

4. **Expand the symbols:** Write a short list of alternative meanings for your main and secondary symbols. Preferably, only three concepts for each (main symbol: "I see my anger as an eagle flying high in the sky," "like a speeding train," and "my anger is an exciting place in the jungle"). (Secondary symbol: "Tranquility is watching a sunset," "reading a book," and "swinging in a hammock.")

5. **Structure the ritual:** Once we are clear about the emotions, the corresponding symbols, and their alternatives, we must imagine the characteristics of time and space, objects, and even mantras we want to integrate into our ritual. Note: It is important that the personal ritual has a flexible and relatively simple structure, so that it can be repeated as many times as necessary. For example, if I have to drive to Acapulco to perform my ritual and I live in Mexico City, it will be hard to reproduce. So, in consultation with my patients, we come up with a simplified format for the ritual and perform it in the office, so that they can carry it out within the context of their daily lives.

6. **Representative objects and mantras:** These are all things that have symbolic value and support the execution of the ritual. Representative objects are chosen based on the symbols and emotions we want to work on. Here we can connect the representative object and the mantra that describes its meaning, along with the evocation we want to generate—the ritual is a physical mantra in motion. Continuing with our example, maybe the objects we want to include for our ritual are matches, candle, photograph of an eagle, sound of river water previously recorded on the cell phone, to name a few. Once we have gathered the elements of our ritual, we think of some mantras that describe our intention with the object and the evocation of its meaning.

[11] C.G. Jung Page (2003). http://www.cgjungpage.org/. Accessed March 9, 2023.

7. **Intuitive ceremony:** According to Jung, intuition is "the psychic function that perceives the inherent possibilities of the present moment and closely relates to the unconscious."[11] To reach this ceremonial moment, we have already made a journey of introspection and reflected on all the elements involved in our ritual. The planning process is a ritual in itself, but it is now, in this step, when it takes form on stage that the symbolic content will emerge. Since the symbols contain an energetic charge by themselves, the development of the ritual will appear organically and spontaneously, according to the script or agenda we previously established.

8. **Repetition of the ritual:** This is an aspect that will depend on the purpose and intention with which the ritual was created. There are cases where doing it once is enough, and others where it needs to be done periodically. In the therapeutic context, it is performed only once; that is, the structured format for that ritual is not repeated but new ones can be created. People who are not in therapy can repeat it as often as necessary. It is recommended that it be something simple and meaningful, so that it can be easily reproduced and included in daily life.

## Clinical Case: Encounter

Fabiola came to therapy because she was going to move to another country due to her husband's work. She was happy living in Mexico City, where she had a group of friends, activities, a house, and routines that gave her stability, and was reluctant to move to another country, even though she needed to do so. She had already moved from California to Mexico, and felt that for the first time she "had a stable home."

For a year and a half, we worked on the triggers and fears she had about moving to another country, which led us to touch on her childhood wound. When she was little, her parents argued intensely and her father was alcoholic and violent. Her mother also asked her to hide in the closet to listen to the conversations he had with his lover and then report back. She felt unprotected and at the same time responsible for being the intermediary between her parents, to "give stability" to her home.

The move meant that, once again (as in her childhood), she would have to be the pillar of her family. She had assembled a group of people who helped her "manage her life": her chauffeur, who drove her around as she had difficulty with driving; her daughter's nanny, who was her right hand; and her friends, who gave her a sense of belonging. Losing the camaraderie that gave her peace and stability immediately connected her with her abandonment and loneliness wound, along with the fear of taking on the responsibility without feeling the ability to do so.

When Fabiola was able to put into words the emotions from her childhood and their meanings, we began to work on different alternatives for her, moving forward. She realized that she was not just a survivor but also a warrior of her own personal story, since she had the ability from a young age to understand her family situation and take charge of solving "what was happening there." She also discovered that she felt exhausted from being alone solving life and that the move meant returning to that dark place of her childhood.

Together, we observed the potential triggers that could present themselves for her in her new place of residence. First, in order to deal with traveling for long distances or driving on urban beltways, we mapped out routes in her new city where she would feel comfortable. Second, we reviewed the symbolic content of this situation where "traveling on her own" represented a new and different way of taking responsibility for herself in adulthood, and not just another version of abandonment and responsibility toward her parents.

We also created mantras to use when she felt stressed, worried, fearful, or tired, to bring her back to the present and detach her from the triggers that could take her to her childhood wound.

Finally, she moved. Several weeks passed, and as we continued our meetings over Zoom, she talked about her difficulty in adapting and feelings of deep nostalgia and grief. She missed everything she had left in Mexico. And worst of all, the echoes from her childhood were haunting her again. She and her husband had bought a nice, spacious house with a garden and a pool, but she felt alienated and out of place there.

One day, during our video call, she shared that she felt incredibly sad. As she did so, I observed everything around her: a sunny day, her green garden, the colorful and lush flowers she had planted, a relaxing silence that distanced her from the hustle and bustle of a busy city, and sun rays illuminating her face and her jet-black hair. Everything in front of me was perfect, but she was elsewhere, in that dark tunnel of the past as the present was slipping away.

The beauty of that moment, along with Fabiola who couldn't see it, was the indicator for me to go get her from the past and bring her to the present.

Returning to the emphasis of the title and content of this book, pain should have the ultimate function of preparing us to find new opportunities. If we do not die despite the traumatic past experience, then life is waiting for us to embrace it.

Our wounded discourse can persist for years, even if our reality has changed and we are not in danger. It is this habit that connects us with what we fear most about our wound, thus clouding the vision of who we are now.

Fabiola's present was in that beautiful house.

So I said: "Let's see, give me a tour of your house."

She smiled, wiped her tears, and a flash of joy escaped across her face. Very proudly, she took me through every corner of her new house and explained to me how her family lived in each space.

As I watched her walk through the hallways, climb the stairs, open a door, and pass through French doors, I thought, *This is an ideal moment to create a ritual.*

So, after she had finished showing me her house, I said: "Maybe you need to ask your house for permission to inhabit it and thank it so that you can finally occupy it and feel that you belong to it."

Together we set out to plan the ritual, which turned into a family ceremony. Each family member wrote a letter in which they introduced themselves to the house by saying their name out loud, stating what it meant for them to live there, and asking permission to occupy it, and finishing by expressing gratitude. Each had a lit candle with which they illuminated the spaces, while stroking the objects and contemplating their textures and colors.

Although the initial intention was to perform a personal ritual, Fabiola and I agreed that she would establish the format and then she would invite her husband and daughter to participate in "the activity."

The emotions she wanted to work on were abandonment and loneliness.

"How do these emotions feel inside you?" I asked.

She sighed. "It's like everything is empty and silent."

"And how would that look in the physical world?" I asked.

"It would look dark, with closed doors and without any voice being heard," she replied.

After hearing the main symbol for the structure of her ritual, I started to explore the secondary symbols:

"How would you feel if abandonment and loneliness did not exist?"

She smiled again (like when I asked her to show me her house). "I would feel that there is finally light in my life, that I can use my own voice, and that I can enjoy and share with my family."

"What else?" I added.

She relaxed and said, "Well, I would have friends and find my new place here."

"What objects would you like to symbolize what you just told me?" I asked.

She reflected and said: "I would like to illuminate my house with candles while my husband, my daughter, and I say nice things to it."

Finally, they performed the ceremony and intuitively added new elements to the ritual, such as telling stories and composing a song for the house, elements that had not been initially planned.

When a ritual is performed, energy flows through all the elements with which people participate, connecting with the soul and creating something greater than they had imagined.

# 11

# AMULETS

## Healing and Transcending Objects

Amulets are among the oldest objects used by humanity to ensure good harvests, protect oneself from nature, escape suffering or physical, moral, and spiritual pains, and so on. Some are made of stones, crystals, or carved wood, and selected as special due to their particular shapes or colors.

The inclusion of amulets has grown over time. It started out with people using objects that were inherited from others, belonged to someone else, or were part of an event and conferred a certain power. This makes me think of the collection of small boxes I have acquired in countries I have visited and which symbolize freedom for me, or the ceramic, crystal, or pendant butterflies that act as my good luck charms.

The word amulet comes from the Latin *amuletum*, a word first used in the *Naturalis Historia* written by Pliny the Elder, a Roman writer and military man from the 1st century.[12] It means "an object that protects a person against a problem" and is related to the term "talisman," from the Arabic *tilasm* and Greek *telesma* or *telein*, which means "to initiate someone into the mystery."

Amulets are objects that can be easily carried anywhere. In many cases, they are imbued with the power of supernatural protection, depending on the era, culture, or religion, and have different meanings. For the purposes of this book, although they respond to subtle

---

[12] Pliny The Elder, *Natural History: A Selection* (Penguin Classics, 1991). Pliny the Elder's encyclopedia is a colossal work that sought to cover all the knowledge available at a specific point in time during the Roman Empire, including natural history, geography, mathematics, anthropology, human physiology, and many other fields. It became the model for all future encyclopedias.

differences, I will use the concepts of amulet and talisman as synonyms.

In ancient times as well as the Middle Ages, Jews, Christians, and Muslims living in the East believed in the protective and healing power of amulets and talismans. They were used in three ways:

1. Those worn on the body
2. Those hung or placed over a sick person's bed
3. Those with medicinal qualities

There is evidence that Jews, Christians, and Muslims used their sacred books as talismans in life-or-death situations. Christian authorities have distanced themselves from the use of amulets and other talismans but do endorse the legitimate and correct use of sacraments that correspond to the image of traditional Christianity. [13]

Some representative amulets are:

- **Pentagrams:** Created in the West since the Middle Ages to attract money, health, and love, pentagrams, or pentacles, consist of a metal plate with a five-pointed star; they are also used as a symbol of earth and are one of the figures of sacred geometry. In the Sixth and Seventh Books of Moses, the pentagram contains the Hebrew word *Elohim* at its center, a reference to one of God's names. [14]
- **Magic Squares:** Square tables that include four horizontal columns and four vertical ones, with a series of whole numbers, so that

---

[13] Sacraments are rituals that represent the work of God, and include baptism, confirmation, communion, reconciliation, holy orders, marriage, and anointing of the sick. They are words and actions that confer or increase Divine Grace. Their purpose is the sanctification of humans, the edification of the body of Christ, and worship. They strengthen and nurture faith.

[14] The Sixth and Seventh Book of Moses are magic books supposedly written by Moses. They include the arts of the ancient Hebrews, taken from Kabbalah and Talmud, and contain spells that are said to have been used to create some of the miracles described in the Bible.

- the sum of the numbers by columns, rows, and main diagonals is the same. For philosophical, numerological, and practical reasons, they are used in the Chinese practice of feng shui, or geomancy, as a way of determining orientations and specific spaces. [15]
- **Eye of Providence:** A cabalistic symbol of protection representing God's eye and the Divine Providence that has created the whole universe. It is depicted as a human eye enclosed in a triangle, representing the Holy Trinity in Christianity. This concept of "the all-seeing eye" can be found in other religions and cultures. For Buddhists, it is the Eye of the World, and for Egyptians, the eye of Horus is revered as a symbol of power and protection. Masons use this symbol as a reminder to be mindful of their thoughts and actions since God is always watching. This amulet can be an image or a piece of jewelry.
- **Star of David:** One of the main symbols of Judaism and also of past Hebrew cultures. Its Hebrew name is Magen David. Its inspiration comes from the *Song of Songs*.[16] The star has two interlocked triangles with six points, corresponding to a biblical verse in Judaism that speaks of the intimate relationship between God and humanity: "I am my beloved's, and my beloved is mine." It also represents the union between Heaven and Earth. Since idolatry is prohibited in Judaism, amulets underscore the importance of text and names.
- **Crucifix:** A Christian symbol aimed at promoting the contemplation and understanding of its intrinsic meaning: In the image of the crucified Jesus, the mystery of the death of the Son of God as the supreme act of love, the source of life, and salvation for humanity of all times is revealed. Nowadays, it serves as a protective amulet for many people.

---

[15] Feng shui is an Oriental philosophy based on finding balance and contributing positive energies to the places we inhabit.

[16] The Song of Songs is one of the books of the Old Testament and is unique in the Bible as it does not address divine issues. It narrates the joy of lovers who find complete harmony in their sexual intimacy.

- **Jewish *Tallit*:** A prayer shawl with blue-striped corners and knotted fringes at each corner. It is one of the oldest and most common talismanic objects in the world. It became a perpetual reminder for the wearer to stay within the bounds of decency, morality, and ethics and never forget God's law.
- **Angel Text:** A lesser-known amulet but with a solid base in Jewish tradition. Its Hebrew name is *kimiyah*. It consists of the names of angels or passages from the Bible written on squares of parchment by rabbinic scribes. The parchment is then placed in an ornate silver container and worn somewhere on the body. Muslims also carry such amulets, called *Ta'wiz*, with the chosen text from the Koran. Usually, this is selected depending on the situation for which the amulet is designed. The use of amulets and other talismans is considered superstitious by more radical Muslims.
- **Rosaries:** Objects formed by a series of strung beads that commemorate 20 mysteries (15 in the traditional form) of the life of Jesus Christ and the Virgin Mary, reciting one Lord's Prayer after announcing each of them, 10 Hail Marys, and a Glory. The Church considers this prayer effective for the most difficult causes.
- **Chinese Amulets:** There are different symbols to promote good luck that take various forms. In ancient Chinese tradition, the fu symbol of good fortune was hung on the main door during the Spring Festival and Chinese New Year. This practice started in 256 BC, during the Zhou dynasty, to prevent the goddess of poverty from entering homes.
- **Imperial Dragon:** In China, the Imperial Dragon represents the emperor as a direct descendant of the Dragon. This symbol is found throughout their architecture with meanings of protection, strength, prosperity, and wisdom.
- **Buddhist Amulets:** *Srung* are protective amulets that have been used by Vajrayana Buddhists for centuries. They are created from Mandala and Yantra traditions for specific challenges and elimination of obstacles, sufferings, or ills experienced by people. Their shape and content are made according to the lineage text and the goal sought to be achieved. It must be prepared by a teacher,

or *lama*, with the special blessing of blessed substances varying, depending on their purpose, and also must be consecrated with the recitation of the mantra and hand position (*mudra*). The amulet is wrapped in cloth and worn around the neck. Similarly, engraved cylinders containing precious stones can be placed at house entrances.

- **Mezuzah:** The Hebrew word denotes a parchment inscribed with two verses from the Torah.[17] It is placed inside a case attached to the right doorframe of the entrance to homes and also interior doors. It is one of the most distinctive features of Jewish homes and one of the oldest and most deeply rooted precepts of Judaism. People use it as an amulet of protection for their families. Every seven years, the cases must be opened, and the texts reviewed by rabbis. If any letter from the text is erased, the parchment must be replaced with a new one.

It is believed that you must check Mezuzah parchments when there is illness in the house, bad luck in business, or conflicts with children or partners.

For example, a Jewish family had a son who frequently fell ill. They consulted several doctors, but none could provide a definitive diagnosis. So, they sought advice from a rabbi.

"Have you checked the mezuzot?" he asked.

Seven years had passed since their last parchment review, so they proceeded to check them with a specialized scribe.

The Hebrew word *briut*, meaning "health in all areas of life: mental, spiritual, and physical," was found to be erased, as was the word *guf*, meaning "body."

The family replaced the scroll with a new one and returned to see the doctor, who ordered a specific study and discovered that the boy had Addison's disease (a disorder of the adrenal glands).

---

[17] The Torah refers to the five sacred books of the Jewish Law, supposedly written by Moses under divine inspiration. They are: Genesis-Bereshit (In the Beginning), Exodus-Shemot (Names), Leviticus-Veikré (And He called), Numbers, and Deuteronomy.

Subsequently, the scribe contacted the family to say he had reviewed the scroll again and found several words with the letter "a" erased. In many cases, it is found that complete words or the numerical significance of certain letters that appear erased correspond to the issue the family is experiencing.

## Therapeutic Amulets: My Methodology

At this point in our journey, I find it relevant to mention that the therapeutic tools I have presented here—mantras, rituals, and amulets—are elements whose relevance is due to their practical use and collective wisdom, but above all, the various qualities they possess for healing. For almost 30 years, my area of work has focused on the beliefs, will, and creative and natural capacity of human beings to bring forth their inner world into form. It is in this sense that I have utilized the foundation of these ancient practices combined with my therapeutic approach.

In modern medicine, we know that much of the "magical" character attributed to panaceas for curing various ailments is based on the laws of nature.[18] As mentioned earlier, among the multiple purposes of an amulet, is to protect people against diseases. Pliny the Elder designated them as objects or medical elements capable of acting directly or indirectly on a person's health.

What in the past were considered "curses" or "hexes" we now call "disease," and the ways of addressing it have evolved with scientific advances and continuous additions to our human knowledge, but what activates the will and strength of the spirit remains a mystery.

Another unresolved mystery is what determines that the same external experience affects people differently who have lived through it simultaneously (for example: two siblings experiencing violence from their alcoholic parents. One becomes addicted to drugs and suffers from depression; the other decides to leave home, pursue a career, and work).

---

[18] Panaceas are remedies, solutions, or medicines that solve any kind of problem. They are believed to cure many illnesses.

There are so many factors coexisting in a person's psychic, physical emotional, and intellectual life that it is impossible to know exactly what has determined their attitude toward life. This is what I would consider the magic and mystery of modern times.

My grandmother was diagnosed with terminal cancer and given three months to live. She received treatment in the United States, and her doctor only spoke English. My father accompanied her to the consultation and translated into Spanish what "the doctor said about her health condition and treatment." The session went like this:

"Your mother has invasive cancer and has three months to live," the doctor said. ("Mom, the doctor says you're already healthy, that you're cured, and you have a whole life ahead of you," translated my father.)

"We will apply chemotherapy and radiation to lessen the pain." ("They will give you treatment to strengthen you and help you recover your vitality. And that's all, Mom," my father told her.)

My grandmother went on to live an additional 20 years. This is something that science cannot explain, nor can I, but I believe that the combination of elements I have mentioned was the "magic potion" she needed for her recovery.

Despite a clear and existing body of therapeutic work, each time a patient comes to me, I know that I am about to discover a new universe; therefore, the process of planning and preparing therapeutic tools is not standardized in the sense of acting like a recipe, but instead, is adapted from each of these universes.

I have never created the same mantra, ritual, or amulet for different patients because the effectiveness of these tools is determined by the individual and spiritual ingredient the person has contributed to this "magic formula" to heal themselves. At this point, it is also fair to say that I have never achieved the healing of a patient without their will. It is the willingness with which they engage in their process that makes the tools work.

Amulets are, therefore, a therapeutic tool I use with the patient, resulting from a prior elaboration of introspection and deep analysis of their emotions, beliefs, and thoughts. In the exercise and clinical case, I present below, I will describe how this process occurs.

## Creating a Personal Amulet

Amulets are tools that can be combined with mantras. A ritual can also be performed during the planning and creation of an amulet to compact the psychic content within the object. This is how I create amulets together with my patients. Not everyone who has an amulet undergoes a process around it. That may be because it is an object acquired from someone else, or simply found or bought as a souvenir of an important moment that connected them with an emotion, belief, spiritual meaning, or thought they wish to evoke through the object.

Here are the five steps for planning and creating an amulet within therapy:

1. **Detecting an Emotional Need:** People connect to our reality through the senses: visual, olfactory, auditory, gustatory, and tactile. Our predominant sense is the one that connects us to the present moment, and we can use it as the base element for our amulet. (For example, if the predominant sense is smell, the amulet could be a small bottle containing oil or essence; if it is auditory, the amulet could contain a small bell or any other object that emits a sound.) The detection of our emotional need is done by paying attention to a situation we have repeatedly experienced without being able to resolve it. We reflect on the emotion that would help us transcend that situation. (For example, a person who usually speaks in public always gets nervous beforehand, so they turn their ring (amulet) a couple of times to center themselves, feel confident, and start speaking. In my case, I take a sip from a glass of water before giving a talk.)
2. **Choosing the Amulet Material:** This choice should be based on the characteristics of the emotion we want to evoke. (For example, if I want to remember to be "tougher or assertive," and my predominant sense is touch, then I choose a rough material like sandpaper or rope and not a soft one like velvet or silk.) The material should have symbolic content that refers to a belief, memory, or thought that supports the amulet's purpose. (For example, I might choose a rough material resembling a sackcloth from my grandmother to remind me of her strong character.)

3. **Accompanying the Mantra:** The mantra (see the mantra exercise) is crafted based on the symbolic content we want the object to represent. Preferably, it should be a phrase no longer than five words; for example, "Tough as my grandmother."
4. **Ritual for the Amulet:** It begins with the initial reflection on the emotion and how it relates to the selection of the object's material and passes through the mantra. The ritual itself occurs when it is put into action. At this point, it is important to observe if all elements correspond with what we want to evoke; if something does not make sense, we can eliminate or modify it. It is an intuitive process, whereby the unconscious will indicate how and where we should direct ourselves. To maintain the intention and psychic energy with which we have charged the object, it is important that others not touch it, and if possible, do not explain it to others, as they will not be able to understand its significance, so the energy will be dispersed. When we allow external thoughts to interfere, we stop honoring our process. In his book *Breaking the Habit of Being Yourself: How to Lose Your Mind and Create a New One*, Dr. Joe Dispenza, a researcher in neurology, neuroscience, biochemistry, and cellular biology, expresses it like this: "Prove to yourself that you are a divine creator. We should never wait for science to give us permission to do something unusual. Let's be brave enough to look at our lives, do something unheard of, and repeat it again and again. True empowerment comes when we start to analyze our beliefs deeply."
5. **Decide the Time and Space:** Perhaps the purpose of our amulet is designed for specific situations, or maybe we have chosen for it to accompany us all the time. In any case, it is important that every time we carry it, we remember the intention for which it was created.

## Clinical Case: Breaking Pacts

I recall being struck by *The Castle of Purity*, a Mexican film based on real events from the 1950s.[19] The movie won five Ariel Awards, Mexico's film industry top awards, including Best Picture. I must have been 15 years old when I watched it, and I questioned whether the story had been invented, as I found it impossible to believe it was true.

The film's plot revolves around a man named Gabriel Lima, a manufacturer and vendor of rat poison who is obsessed with purity of body and spirit. He is convinced that the outside world is harmful to his family and decides to lock up his wife Beatriz and their three children for 18 years.

The protagonist describes his worldview this way: "With rats, I have learned to know men; they are the same, which is why I don't want you to have any contact with the world. It's better for you to stay here, among my rats, than to see the best of those out there." The perversion he sought to control in the outside world was lived within his house through violence and incest.

Decades later, a similar story appeared in my office, when I had the opportunity to treat three sisters over different years. With the youngest of them, I created an amulet to break pacts.

Silvia came to me primarily for issues with open-space phobias, night terrors, difficulties in completing her professional projects, as well as trouble forming and keeping relationships. As we delved into her past, she had vague memories of "feeling a presence" in the darkness of night. She was afraid to sleep alone, so she would go to her older sister's bed for protection. However, the nighttime fear did not cease—she would scream, feel disoriented, and have an intense need to be cared for.

This defined her childhood, a constant feeling of danger without understanding the source of the fear, which led to insomnia in adulthood. She also had an older brother who was physically and verbally abusive, and all the sisters feared him immensely.

---

[19] *The Castle of Purity*. Written by Arturo Ripstein and José Emilio Pacheco. Filmoteca UNAM. Mexico City, Mexico, 1972. Accessed March 12, 2023.

From a young age, Silvia was cheerful and direct in her expressions. Her mother considered her rebellious and was uncomfortable with Silvia confronting her with questions and asking for explanations about their way of living, to which her mother would reprimand her by saying, "If you keep on being the way you are, no one will love you, and you will end up alone."

Her father would leave the house for periods without any explanation, a situation no family member was allowed to question. Consequently, her mother lived in a state of depression, neglected domestic chores, and showed no affection towards her children. Their parents believed that "the world was evil, women could be raped, and one should distrust everybody."

In time, Silvia remembered that "the presence" was her older brother entering the room at night to sexually abuse her sisters. No one talked about it, and she did not know if she had imagined it or if it was real. Her mother knew what was happening but refused to admit it; instead, she supported her son's violent behavior and blamed her daughters for provoking him.

Years later, Silvia moved in with one of her sisters, where she continued the routine of sleeping in the same bed. She felt fearful and dependent, unable to become independent and feeling guilt and indebtedness to her sisters for protecting her from abuse.

Every time she tried to undertake a personal project, she found herself unable to complete it. She felt inadequate without a partner and believed that her mother's childhood sentence of ending up alone had come true.

Eventually, Silvia rented her own apartment, traveled a bit, and settled into a job, but the guilt and debt she felt towards her sisters persisted. We worked on this, along with her difficulty in having a partner, and explored why she did not feel happy in her profession. In one session, she told me she had received recognition at her company and had been promoted. As she said this, I observed that her face was filled with suffering.

"Your words don't match your expression," I said.

"Excuse me?" she said, indignantly.

I smiled slightly. "You're saying you've just received something you've worked years for, and your face tells me it's the worst thing that has happened to you."

"I can't be happy," she said.

"Why is that?"

"Because my sisters sacrificed themselves for me," she said.

Time to make an amulet, I thought. Silvia needed something physical to bring her back to the present from that childhood room.

"You need something to remind you that you are all adults now," I said. "Putting your life on hold won't repair the harm done to them. You weren't the one who betrayed them."

"How can I let go of the guilt? Let go of them?" she asked as she wiped away tears.

"By giving them back their story."

I handed her a notebook.

"Write down your feelings here, knowing it's not your story," I said.

"I feel like thanking them for protecting me and wishing them well," she said.

"You mean like blessings? Would you tell them, or would you like to give them something?" I asked.

"I want to do something symbolic."

I reminded her of our previous discussion about amulets and suggested that this was a good moment to create one. She decided to make bracelets for her sisters that would include a mantra and blessings.

She bought fine colored threads and wove the bracelets. As she made them, she spoke aloud the following mantra: "The pact is over, blessing between us." The words for her mantra came from doing the mantra exercise described earlier.

It's important to note that her guilt stemmed from an unspoken pact with her sisters to not abandon them. This was why she sabotaged her projects, as they represented disloyalty toward her family simply for feeling happy and independent.

Survivor's syndrome is a mental condition that occurs when a person feels they have done wrong by surviving a traumatic event others did not. Symptoms include chronic anxiety, sleep problems, loss of initiative, poor social adaptation, distrust, uncertainty, anger, and guilt—symptoms my patient had.

Her perception that surviving her brother's abuse, thanks to her sisters' protection and sacrifice, was wrong, prevented her from enjoying her life and focusing on her achievements.

This syndrome has been observed in survivors of the Titanic, concentration camps during the Holocaust, atomic bombs in Hiroshima and Nagasaki, the Vietnam War, and currently, the COVID-19 pandemic.

Returning to the bracelets—the blessings Silvia included for each of her sisters were specific healing wishes related to their difficulties. When she gave them the bracelets, she said she had made them with much love and good wishes, and her relationship with her sisters improved.

How could I anticipate the outcome? Do I use magic instead of therapy? Yes and no. It's due to the well-established therapeutic methodology that the shift in perception and action occurs. At this point, it's fair to share the explanation.

As in all approaches I've mentioned, the work with symbolic aspects of emotions and thoughts, and their connection with emotional wounds, forms a crucial starting point. When a person can decipher the intrinsic meanings of their soul, they can see the motivations behind their actions and take control of their present.

Silvia needed to change her relationship with her sisters internally, let go of her unconscious pact, stop offering her life as a sign of gratitude, and differentiate herself from them through blessings. Everything, absolutely everything, was worked through and contained in the bracelets. That's why I know when an amulet will work.

12

# JOURNALS

## Bearing Witness

A personal journal is something an individual writes privately in a blank notebook about their life, and reflections on it. It's a fragmented text that records the dates on which entries were made. It's also a kind of autobiography, which describes life events, perceptions, emotions, thoughts, or value judgments one has about them. Additionally, it serves to explore the mind and unblock afflictions by handwriting.

People generally write in their journals in the morning, at night, or when they've had a deep and spontaneous reflection. Some people do it in a disciplined manner as a routine. I think of it more as a type of meditation, as it is developed in silence, solitude, and its content is intimate.

## Persepolis, the Age of Enlightenment, and Nü Shu

During Classical Antiquity (800 BC–AD 500), it was common to keep a chronological record. In Persepolis, the first journals found had been written on clay tablets that documented the weather, astronomy, and commercial transactions. [20]

Later, during the Renaissance of the Middle Ages, personal records gained in importance, as people began to reflect on the relationship between man and the universe and the need to preserve memories for

[20] Persepolis was the capital of the ancient Persian Empire, built under Darius I, around 521 BC. It had monumental buildings symbolizing the unity and diversity of the Persian Empire under the Achaemenid Dynasty, as well as the legitimacy of the royal power and the greatness of the kingdom.

future generations. Furthermore, paper became more widespread as a writing material, being much more accessible compared to parchment. Travel diaries also became more important, as journeys to distant countries were unusual.

The Enlightenment was a cultural and intellectual movement in Europe that began in the mid-18th century and promoted profound social and cultural changes until the outbreak of the French Revolution. It was called the Age of Enlightenment because its vision and influence impacted the scientific, economic, political, and social realms of the time. [21] This thought was transmitted to the populace by writers who created new ways of understanding reality, and the narrative of personal journals began to change as a result of this influence.

*Nü Shu*, a Chinese term meaning "women's writing," is the only language in the world exclusive to women and features unique calligraphy and meanings. It emerged in the 13th century in Jiangyong, a rural province of Hunan in China, and is derived from Chinese characters adapted to the local dialect (*Chegguan Tuhua*) but with oblique instead of square strokes and elements, such as vertical but inclined and arched lines.

*Nü Shu* was shared secretly through writing on fans or embroidering on handkerchiefs. Its female script highlighted themes such as love, suffering, fears, and desires through letters, poems, songs, or phrases. It was a language transmitted from mothers to daughters and functioned as both a personal and collective diary.

The first object hinting at this script's existence is a bronze coin from the time of the Taiping Heavenly Kingdom (1851–1860), a rebel kingdom that brought about social reforms like gender equality. It bears an inscription of eight characters. Another (more literal) translation of *Nü Shu* is "all women under heaven belong to the same family."

---

[21] The Age of Enlightenment is a period in history characterized by the fight against ignorance through the "lights" of knowledge and reason. Its features included a sense of faith in progress, the search for happiness, the sovereignty of reason, the evidence of the senses as the sources of learning, and the rising of ideals such as liberty, equality, and the separation of Church and State.

## Journals in Literature

Various writers have used their journals for different purposes, such as narrative strategies, tools to connect more intimately with readers, blending them with fiction, or integrating them within the epistolary genre (letters), for example.

Some personal testimonies that describe a particular era have resonated over time, such as *The Diary of Anne Frank*. Anne was a young Dutch Jewish girl who wrote about her life during the two years she hid in the attic of her house with her family to avoid capture by the Nazis during World War II. They hid there from June 12, 1942 until August 1, 1944, when they were discovered and taken to the Bergen-Belsen concentration camp, where Anne then died of typhus at the age of 15.

Anne wrote three books that are still preserved in the Anne Frank House Museum on Prinsengracht Street in central Amsterdam. She attributed human traits to her diary, such as the patience she had lost in the hiding place with her family, saying, "Paper is more patient than people." Writing helped her cope with years of confinement. She named her diary Kitty, an imaginary friend to whom she wrote letters about her dreams, fears, hopes, and experiences in the refuge.

Franz Kafka used a blend of fiction and personal testimony in his novella *The Metamorphosis*, whose plot centers on Gregor Samsa, a man who transforms into an insect. Kafka also documented his life in his *Diaries* (1910–1923), which reveal his tormented personality, concerns, and secrets. Kafka instructed his friend Max Brod to burn his writings after his death, but Max disregarded this wish and published them.

In the second of her journals, *As Consciousness Is Harnessed to Flesh: Journals and Notebooks*, 1964–1980, writer and film director Susan Sontag recounted her travels to Sweden, Hanoi, and the Vietnam War and explained her political and moral awakening through her emotions and reflections.

In *Intimate Diaries*, Spanish writer and philosopher Miguel de Unamuno shared the spiritual crisis he experienced during the late 19th century. His diaries consist of five notebooks in which he narrated his feelings, doubts, hopes, and fears.

In *The War*, French novelist, screenwriter, and film director Marguerite Duras narrated the last days of the Nazi occupation of France and the first days of its liberation, along with her personal story.

In his short story *Diary of a Madman*, Russian writer and playwright Nikolai Gogol used the diary as a narrative strategy to let the reader see what is happening in the narrator's mind. By telling his own story, he sought to create a bond with the reader. This story was adapted into a 1963 film in the United States and has also been performed as a play in theaters around the world.

In the intimate diaries of Alejandra Pizarnik, one finds reflections on her Jewish heritage and her difficulty adapting to different environments due to a history of persecution and distrust. She narrates how she became interested in Zionism during her adolescence, writing on July 24, 1955: "My mother wants to send me to Israel for a year (her intuition always on point: at 12, I was a Zionist)."

## Progoff's Intensive Journal: My Methodology

As discussed earlier, the Progoff Intensive Journal method is the most comprehensive tool for deep personal journaling I know of, as it covers all aspects of a person. I consider it highly effective, due to its theoretical basis for deciphering symbolic language, developing freedom and creativity, and exploring one's own life.

It is different from the commonly used journal because its structure is designed for introspection and finding meaning or solutions to our themes and experiences. In private consultations, I choose various exercises for patients to complete their journal entries ("entry" refers to each new page or reflection undertaken, along with the date it is made).

Implementing all of Progoff's strategies to explore the unconscious or soul's language would be impossible; even I haven't accomplished this in my own journal. However, some approaches can be undertaken for a more complete journaling experience.

This methodology is definitively for self-reflection. Anything written in the journal will have a therapeutic purpose, whether the person is in therapy or not. In Progoff's words:

> "Each person is committed to finding the way of life and the form of being that is faithful to their own nature. When our attention focuses on the inner self within the total context of our life, all the resources of deep knowing become accessible to us. People are sensitive to the threads of their inner life when they have a defined way of working with them. The Journal becomes a companion, a portable alter-ego, an intimate friend that will discuss and debate with the person the decisions of their life through a dialogue. The Intensive Journal is our internal workshop, the place where we creatively shape the artwork of our life. The Intensive Journal's workbook is specifically designed to provide a tool through which people can discover within themselves resources they did not know they possessed. The meaning of life must then be experienced by the person. The method provides an indirect approach to resolving our life problems by moving inward and encountering them on a deeper level."

The journal's structure (provided in a binder during workshops worldwide) has 21 sections. Each represents an independent aspect of life or an introspective or meditative way to connect with internal and symbolic information (refer to the Mantra Crystals section to see the modules). I will simply mention the sections that compose the Intensive Journal to demonstrate the comprehensive structure it offers and the various approaches to addressing life themes:

- **Life Period Log**
- **Daily Log**
- **Dialogue Dimension** – with people, with work, with society, and with the body
- **Deep Dimension** – dream log, expanding dreams, twilight imagery log, extending imagery, dialogue with inner wisdom
- **Life/Time Dimension** – life story log, life crossroads log, life intersection and now

- **Meaning Dimension** – meditation log, connections, mantra crystals, depths and explorations, testament

In the exercise and patient case, I will provide a clear overview of how to use a journal for therapeutic purposes. By "therapeutic," I mean the healing capacity we all possess.

## Journaling as an Introspective Tool

By itself, writing is an intimate and sacred act, as silence helps us evoke our creative capacity and allows inspiration to surface (inspiration means "the spirit that resides within me"). I have discovered that the soul also needs to be exercised through reflection, meditation, dream observation, careful word usage, exploration of symbols, forgiveness, compassion, and various other aspects. When we experience these, we feel part of something larger than ourselves.

The key to making this introspective journey is to observe and bear witness to everything that happens to us, paying attention and intuitively recording the information we receive from the deepest places within. We don't need to interpret or judge what is revealed to us, but rather, absorb it and integrate it into the consciousness of our present—again, and again, and again.

"Write as if no one is watching," I tell my patients in order to encourage them to say everything they need to say. "The journal and I will keep your secrets."

Although my patients laugh, they know it's true: we feel so alienated, invaded, and without privacy that we have forgotten—or do not know or dare not connect with—ourselves. If we are fortunate enough to do so sincerely, the fear of disappointing others arises.

How many times have we written something imagining that someone is watching? How many times have we regretted our solitary confessions? How many times have we blamed ourselves for recognizing our deepest feelings?

Working on our journal with discipline entails some challenges: stopping lying to ourselves, committing, not getting distracted, returning to ourselves . . . always to ourselves.

## Steps for Keeping a Personal Journal

1. **Personalizing the Journal:** This means making the notebook in which we write truly our own. It can't be just any notebook. One way to honor our work is to dedicate respect and time to it. We should think carefully about the characteristics we want our journal to have. It could be one with lined or blank pages, of letter or standard size, and most importantly, what cover it will have (we can use clippings, photographs, or phrases to decorate it). This selection can be the initiation ritual for our journal. We can also give it a title if we feel comfortable, just as Anne Frank did with her diary, which she called "Dear Kitty" and to which she wrote: "I hope I will be able to confide everything to you, and I hope you will be a great source of comfort and support" (June 12, 1942). I remember my youth journals were golden with a hard cover, but what fascinated me most was their lock.

2. **Choosing the Space and Time**: For writing in our journal, we must select a quiet and private space, preferably a place with a door that we can close to "inform the world that we are not available," as my teacher Ethel Krauze says. To strengthen the purpose of the journal, we should schedule the times when we will sit down to write (I will later talk about Julia Cameron's "Morning Pages"). We can also add elements to harmonize the environment, such as a candle or incense. Discipline, patience, and perseverance are fundamental in order to allow our unconscious language to surface and reveal itself more. In my experience, the more I write, the more dreams I recall; and the more I recall, the more I understand the meaning of unconscious symbols and consciously translate them into my life. It's like having a puzzle box without a picture on the cover and assembling it intuitively until the form appears.

3. **Choosing the Reflection Theme:** Entries in our journal should have a concrete intention. We need to be careful in choosing the theme and how to approach it. Here, I share some entries to develop fluidly; it's important to avoid value judgments or analyzing what we are about to write. Simply let the pen go and see where it leads. By doing so, we allow the symbolic language to appear, guided only by our intuition. The entries (including reflections on personal history, present perception, and future projection) are:

- Your childhood or adulthood (can be a specific memory)
- Difficulties or challenges in your life (past or present)
- Important memories or secrets you haven't shared (they can also be others' secrets and how you feel knowing and keeping them)
- People who influence your life the most
- Actions you are proud of or regret
- A dream and why it caught your attention
- A journey
- Your relationship with your body
- Your current relationships
- Your job
- Spiritual experiences
- Gratitude
- Your future goals
- The unknown
- Death
- Love or hate and what they mean to you
- An inner wisdom dialogue with an important figure
- A dialogue with a situation
- Your legacy for when you leave this world

4. **Letting the Energy Settle:** It's important not to read what we've written for a couple of days to ensure the energy doesn't disperse and the unconscious remains active externally. If we want to revisit a pending theme, we should write from where our intuition indicates, without planning or controlling our words.
5. **Reading Aloud:** After two weeks, we can read some entries aloud paying attention to our breathing and tone of voice. Speak slowly and observe if any ideas emerge. If so, we note them next to the phrase and date it. This gives us an idea of how the information has transformed or what new alternatives have manifested.
6. **Expressing Gratitude:** When we finish writing, we should thank our journal for its receptivity and companionship and then store it in a safe place. By establishing a relationship with the object, we imbue it with energy that helps us continue with our purpose. In this way, the journal also becomes an amulet.

## Personal Case: Dialoguing with Janusz Korczak

I had been searching for my Progoff Intensive Journal binder for a couple of weeks because I wanted to share an exercise I did during a course in England. It had simply disappeared. I looked for the binder in all the logical places and found nothing.

I decided to let a couple of weeks pass to see if I could recall anything. One morning, I searched again, opening drawers, looking in bookshelves, the wardrobe, suitcases . . . Still nothing.

My resolve didn't waver. I couldn't let go of the idea that this part of the book needed to contain the intact exercise as I wrote it during the course in order to preserve the text's soul and energy.

Then I used a technique from the Silva Method that I learned in a course during my youth.[22] I took a deep breath to clear my mind and asked myself, *Why isn't my journal in the obvious places?* I kept exploring while breathing, but still no answer emerged.

Next, I decided to ask Korczak: "Do you want to appear in my book or not?" (This is an adjustment I've added to my personal work, which involves connecting with something or someone and dialoguing.) And like a ray of light falling on my head, I got the answer: *You hid the binder along with your journals so no one would see it.*

Indeed, I went to that spot, and there it was. This is how the continued work of intuition and symbolism functions. The Silva Method helped me make a mental regression (going to the place where one last left the object or the space where one was), but I couldn't remember it because "the obvious" didn't match the place I had symbolically chosen to store (hide) the binder.

Understanding the relationship of deep meaning to everyday things is a practice I regularly invite my patients to do. Once again, it might seem like a "magical act," but it involves many psychological processes.

---

[22] The Silva Method consists of mental exercises set in a progressive fashion, aiming to efficiently use mental abilities. José Silva was a Mexican-American parapsychologist and writer, and the creator of the Silva Method for Mind Control.

Polish pediatrician and educator Janusz Korczak was a significant historical figure.[23] I don't remember when I first heard of him, but his story moved and fascinated me. I thoroughly researched his various biographies, along with texts and essays. *I would have loved to have been his student*, I thought.

When I decided to search intuitively, and in some way "ask for help and permission" from Janusz Korczak, the physical place and what it symbolized (a hiding place) became clear in my mind.

One night, Korczak appeared in my dream and said: "I want you to write a story about my children—a story about me."

"Who am I to speak of you? Many have already said everything," I replied.

"You will know which story to tell," he said as he faded away.

Days later, articles, a play, a couple of movies, and even an advertisement on a bus about him appeared everywhere.

A year later, I took a trip to Poland to march through the concentration and extermination camps in an annual event called The March of the Living, where people from all over the world come together to honor Holocaust victims and follow the route once known as The Death March.[24]

In the Treblinka extermination camp,[25] there's a vast field with stones shaped like tombstones carved with the names of the

---

[23] Janusz Korczak (1879–1942) was a Polish and Jewish pediatrician, writer, publicist, social activist and army officer. He was a pioneer in the fight for children's rights and children's equality. He was the director of Warsaw's Dom Sierot Jewish Orphanage, where he taught children a system of self-government, raising their own voices and even printing their own newspaper. During the Nazi occupation he protected and hid 200 children, until he was finally captured and deported with them to the Treblinka Camp, where they were all murdered.

[24] The Death March was the route taken by the Nazis, when they forced concentration camp prisoners to walk long distances without any food or water.

[25] Treblinka was a concentration camp built and operated by Nazi Germany in Poland during World War II. It is estimated that approximately 845,000 Jews were exterminated there.

deceased, and among them is that of Janusz Korczak.Due to the vastness of the place, it was impossible to find his marker, so I walked for a couple of minutes, then stopped and took a breath.

"Do you want me to find you?" I asked.

A slight breeze made me turn right, and there it was.

At this point in my narration, I want to clarify that my intention in sharing this story is to convey that the potential of the human being in intuition, intellect, spirituality, and emotions is inexhaustible. One just needs to dare to discover it.

When we are in touch with our inner selves, we are also connected with everything that exists outside, whether we can see it or not. Today, there are scientific studies on realities our senses cannot perceive but animals can. For example, bats hunt insects through the sound they emit when they fly, which is inaudible to us.

Thus, our perception capacity expands when we have greater inner connection. In the POLIN Museum, which houses the History of Polish Jews, situated where the old Warsaw Ghetto once stood, I was looking at an exhibition about Korczak. Suddenly, a couple behind me began discussing in Spanish that they knew a survivor who had been in the orphanage where Korczak worked. The soul of the character kept speaking to me, or in psychological terms: my intuition was attuned to the world.

Two years later, while taking the Progoff Intensive Journal course in England, I wrote the exercise for the Inner Wisdom Dialogue, which is one of the sections of the Deep Dimension (dream log, dream expansion, twilight imagery log, image extension, dialogue with inner wisdom).

This is an exercise that we can develop in our personal journal, and it serves to evoke our inner wisdom using various figures or historical personalities. For instance, we choose a historical or literary figure whom we believe can understand what we are going through to be our guide and give us advice regarding our concerns or to consult on a topic of our interest.

Before each exercise, it is important to take a couple of minutes, close our eyes, connect with our breath, and pay attention to see if an image appears in our mind.

The image that appeared in my mind was a giant human eye turning into a horse (interestingly, for a time, I took part in equine therapy and established a profound relationship with Jacki, a beautiful thoroughbred, whose death I learned about through a dream).

This was my dialogue with Janusz Korczak: (**J.K** corresponds to him, and **G.G**. corresponds to me. Italics indicate a second reading of the text and new observations I discovered):

**October 3, 2019**

**G.G:** I am very pleased to have this space to talk with you. I have never had the opportunity to do so, even though I wrote a novel about you. I would have loved to know you, you know? I would have even liked to be an orphan so that you could be my father and talk to you about how I feel and ask you several questions. And feel the closeness between a father and daughter. While I write, it dawns on me that I decided to talk about a story of orphans living through a holocaust but with the opportunity to be accompanied by a father like you. I try to imagine how in such a terrible moment, suffering could be overcome if one has the love you provided. Tell me, Korczak, where did you get so much love to give to those children?
*(October 3, 2019 – Second reading: I feel the longing for a father who loves me, who does not betray me, who stays, who does not abandon me.)*

**J.K:** It's something you don't think about. I had a conviction, I had no doubts about what I felt and believed. For me, children were the theme of my life. I always had clarity that respecting and loving them is the most important thing an adult can offer, regardless of the adversities that arise.

**G.G:** I consider you a spiritually elevated human being for the way you lived your life with a heroic strength that doesn't exist today. I think you have a special gift, and you gave a message to the world with your example, and I take this opportunity to thank you for it. I share that I am a person who almost never remembers her childhood. I think something is stuck from that time in my life, and that's why I can't remember. I believe my emotional wound started right there. I would like to ask: What do you recommend for connecting with my inner child that is blocked, with that stage of my life that I don't remember?

**J.K:** You can only live today. Love your present, appreciate who you are, and give yourself the respect you weren't given as a child through your respect here and now. Think of yourself as a tender and beautiful child, with good feelings, very joyful and innocent. I would have adored you. And though you would have been special to me, my favorite, I wouldn't have said so. Instead, I would have helped you to rely on yourself, discover your strengths, and care only about your self-recognition, never that of others.
*(October 3, 2019 – Second reading: Lump in my throat. It caused me a lot of emotion. Tears.)*

**G.G:** How can I trust myself? Convince myself that I deserve to love myself?

**J.K:** You must stop expecting recognition from adults. *(October 3, 2019 – Second reading: Oops, that was a lapse. He speaks to the child I was, as if I weren't an adult.)* Stop expecting recognition from people who can't or don't have the responsibility to make you feel good. That's what I tried with the orphanage children: I helped them rely on themselves, use their voice, and never doubt their emotions and thoughts. The most important thing: to feel entitled to claim their place in the world, and not allow injustices from anyone.

**G.G:** How can I be a present mom to my children?

**J.K:** You first have to be your own mom and give yourself what you couldn't receive as a child. Take care of yourself, respect yourself, and strengthen your voice. Fight for your rights. Once you truly do that, your children will feel that energy.

**G.G:** How did you forgive your dad, who went insane and left you alone at 12, with the responsibility of supporting a family?

**J.K:** I had compassion and pity for him. I always missed him.

**G.G:** What should I do with my dad?

**J.K:** Let him go. Return all your energy toward the love you are seeking in and for yourself. That is true forgiveness.

PART THREE

# BEING IN LIFE

## Exercises

# 13

# RECLAIMING YOUR LIFE

"Being in life" has a completely different meaning than surviving it. "Being in life" means having calm days when we are at peace with what we have, we don't have an emotional agenda to resolve a conflict, we feel free to choose our actions, we tell ourselves good stories, we feel happy, we feel love.

There are days when we walk more slowly. We stop. We observe everyday things with different eyes. We feel like we are on a journey. We enjoy the little things. We choose with whom to share our time. We take care of our words, our space, our energy. We take care of our way of being in life.

The Grant Study was a seven-decade study carried out as part of the Harvard Study of Adult Development at Harvard Medical School to deeply investigate everything related to personal happiness. Research began in 1938, when two study groups were selected: one made up of 268 perfectly healthy Harvard University sophomore students and the other of 332 citizens from the outskirts of nearby Boston, Massachusetts, who had no criminal backgrounds. The objective was to analyze, over the years, what happened to these two groups concerning their quality of life and their state of happiness.

The Grant Study (named for the man who funded it, department store magnate W.T. Grant, and directed by Robert Waldinger at Harvard) followed both groups for 60 years, analyzed all measurable or observable variables, such as IQ and their physical and emotional conditions.

The study's conclusions are discussed in two books by George E. Vaillant, professor of Psychiatry at Harvard Medical School: *Adaptation to Life* (1977/1998) and *Aging Well: Surprising Guideposts to a Happier Life from the Landmark Harvard Study of Adult Development* (2003). Vaillant resumed the Grant study in 1966 and in 2013 published a third book: *Triumphs of Experience. The Men of the Harvard*

*Grant Study*, where he shares the conclusions of his research: "The seventy-five years and twenty million dollars spent on the Grant Project point to a single conclusion that can be summed up in three words: Happiness is love."

Another famous study, the *Genetic Studies of Genius*, was carried out by American psychologist Lewis Terman at Stanford University starting in 1921. Known today as the Terman Study of the Gifted, it is the longest-running study in history.

Terman analyzed the evolution of 1528 children, investigating whether high IQ students were more successful in life. He found that high IQ subjects (which he referred to as "Termites") tended to be healthier, taller, and more socially adapted than other children. He suggested that gifted children should be identified early, offered tailored instruction, and have access to specially trained teachers. He also found that while many of his high IQ subjects were very successful, not all fared well and most actually turned out no better than the average; those who ended up being the most successful tended to rate higher on self-confidence, perseverance, and goal-orientation as children.

Terman published a number of books and articles detailing the research he conducted on intelligence and IQ testing. Best known are *The Measurement of Intelligence: An Explanation of and a Complete Guide for the use of the Stanford Revision and Extension of the Binet-Simon Intelligence Scale* (1916); *The Stanford Revision and Extension of the Binet-Simon Scale for Measuring Intelligence* (1917); and *The Gifted Child Grows Up: Twenty-Five Years' Follow-Up of a Superior Group (Genetic Studies of Genius, Vol. 4)* (1947).

Overall, researchers conclude that having a wide network of friends and cultivating them leads to longer life. The warmth we maintain in our relationships gives us health and happiness. Moreover, they observed that people who strive and are more focused on pursuing their goals and are responsible have better health and live longer than others.

They also concluded that children who do not learn to love and trust the people at home have difficulties developing assertiveness, initiative, and autonomy when they are adults, but the damage can be repaired when they have healthy relationships.

The third part of this book is about self-love. Taking opportunities that can bring us happiness and knowing that it is never too late to be in life. Enjoying our existence should be our top priority. But we have to work at it, be brave, and commit. Being happy and at peace requires a lot of discipline.

I have selected some exercises to share in this section. I have verified them in therapeutic practice and my personal life.

14

# A DATE WITH MYSELF

Chosen solitude is a privilege, one where we have the natural desire to be on our own. Imposed solitude leads to loneliness and need of company.

Learning to enjoy being alone is a discipline that leads to happiness, tranquility, and health. Simply, it is a way of loving ourselves.

The difficulty we have in enjoying solitude is that "being alone" generally reminds us of a painful childhood experience where we felt unprotected and fearful. Life gives us opportunities to learn to be alone and also to let go of the wound, which does not mean that we have to put aside our loved ones or withdraw from a social life. What is important is that we can make certain approaches to feel comfortable in solitude—to like ourselves, in short.

When we discover the benefits of spending time alone, we begin to value this space and change the ways we use our time and energy. We realize that we are the only ones who can give meaning to our time in this world.

One way I take care of my solitude is through silent retreats and personal trips. It is interesting to observe the reactions of some people regarding this discipline that I have practiced for many years—astonishment, discomfort, fear, or judgment, but little shared joy and delight. "I could never do that," "I would die before being silent for a day," some say. Very few are curious to explore what "being alone" is about.

I don't give explanations. Nor do I ask for permission. But I do invite people to try it: to discover the wonderful world that awaits them when they find themselves. Solitude also has its rough part, and being isolated can be an overwhelming experience.

I remember my first silent retreat in the middle of the forest. I was in a cabin where I had decided to be alone, to immerse myself in the practice and not have to please anyone, not even with eye contact. It was a very dark night, and the silence was overwhelming. Nothing but my breathing could be heard. It felt as if the world had disappeared, and only my breath remained (because I couldn't even feel my body). It was terrifying for a moment, and I had a panic attack. I had never experienced absolute silence before.

The evidence of my solitude forced me to recover after a few long minutes. *I am the only one who can help myself,* I thought. The days passed, and the tranquility of silence grew.

Enjoying solitude is an experience that each person must explore and discover for themselves. That is why I invariably ask my patients to practice the discipline of the Artist Date, a technique from Julia Cameron's book *The Artist's Way,* which I have adapted for a therapeutic context to guide patients in the enjoyment of solitude. I have also used it with people with codependency problems and those who do not know their life plan or have lost motivation to achieve their goals. In fact, I use it with everyone. The outcome depends on the patients' willingness to carry it out.

Cameron realized that an artist's creative blocks occur because they have disconnected from their inner world and lost inspiration; that is, the spirit that inhabits each of us. She proposes different ways for the artistic flow to return through certain disciplines, one of which is the Artist Date, which I call A Date with Myself.

I will describe this therapeutic discipline in simple steps so that anyone who wants to reconnect with their inner world or reinforce it can use it.

### A Date with Myself

It is important to set dates with ourselves in the same way we schedule any other appointment, either in our electronic calendar or a day planner like mine. (My orthopedist laughs when he sees my day planner and the big shoulder bag I carry it in; he can't believe there are still people in the world who write on paper when technology is so practical.)

Writing on paper has an important neurological effect, as the information is processed more thoroughly; therefore, it is crucial to write in the planner by hand. We need to block out two hours in our schedule, which is the time our weekly date will take. We must commit to ourselves and give ourselves the same consideration we give others. When we make this space, we connect with a part that is always waiting for us: our inner child. That is why we must keep our word and not cancel or make excuses. Keeping our date with ourselves helps us set boundaries with our environment and explore the world alone.

### Choose the Place

A date with ourselves is not meant for running errands we haven't had time to do, such as taking the car to the shop or going to the dry cleaners. No, this is a date where we will venture to go to a place we have never been before, such as a park, a neighborhood, a cafe, or any place where we can walk or simply sit and contemplate the surroundings. After a couple of months, we can choose some places of interest we want to visit, such as a museum (always alone).

### Avoid Distractions

The primary purpose of this discipline is to connect with our inner world. To achieve the objective, it is important to keep our phone off for the two hours the date lasts (do not cheat by putting it on "vibrate"). Another distraction to avoid is contact with people. If we have decided to get a coffee, we just order it without engaging in any conversation. It is surprising the number of distractions that exist today to distance us from who we really are. Some of my patients panic about doing this exercise, while others find it boring or senseless. I ask them: What part of you scares you, bores you, or makes no sense? It is interesting to realize which part of ourselves we fear, bores us, or we want to remove from our lives. It could be a physical trait, a personality trait, or any other thing that makes us uncomfortable or uneasy.

### Impressions

At the end of our date, we should note our impressions, preferably in a notebook (or an electronic notepad . . . oh well!), the emotions, and thoughts we registered, or simply what we observed in our surrounding and the bodily sensations we experienced.

Isabel told me she didn't know how to entertain herself, nor could she come up with ideas for places to visit. She simply didn't know "what to do with herself." But what bothered her the most was that people would see her "alone."

It reminded me when I was 18 and living alone for the first time in England after having to leave Israel following the outbreak of the Gulf War. I stayed with a London family for six months, got a job as a nanny taking care of two babies, and studied English.

During my trips on the Underground (the subway in London), I thought, "Everyone knows that I'm new here." Now I laugh every time to think that I believed that the people in the carriages knew each other and just happened to all be in my carriage at the same time—it was clear that I had never used the subway before. "I'm not part of the 13:00 hrs. Stamford Hill to Westminster group," I thought again.

The same thing happened when I sat down to eat at a communal round table for six in a cafe and people began sitting in the other seats. I felt I had to introduce myself: "Good afternoon. I'm Gina. What's your name?"

The Artist Date exercise helps us discover who we are and what we are made of, and above all to enjoy our place in the world.

Morning Pages is another technique created by Cameron for introspection and self-contact that I have adapted in private consultation as an alternative to the personal journal. It involves a daily commitment to do three pages of unplanned, spontaneous writing in your journal every morning upon awakening.

In Cameron's words, "Many blocked people are, in fact, very powerful and creative personalities, who have been made to feel guilty for their own strengths and gifts."Alice Miller says the same in her book *The Drama of the Gifted Child: The Search for the True Self.* And so do I in this book.

# 15

# CREATING A NEW IDENTITY

Creating a new identity implies that the true one will emerge, the one that didn't have to be modified to survive its emotional wound. (This exercise is linked to the previous one—all of the exercises in Part Three are connected.)

The more time we spend with ourselves, but more importantly, the more we enjoy solitude, the better we can explore the new identity we want to create.

From my perspective, creating a new identity means seeking those aspects of our being that are unique and make us special. It also means uncovering the secrets we keep in our hearts about what we love and have not yet been able to manifest in our life.

When we are in the process of creating a new identity, it is important to experience coherent emotions (order, structure, harmony) that align with our mind and body. If we lie to ourselves, we sacrifice our true selves and distance ourselves from what we want while experiencing incoherent emotions like fear, uncertainty, sadness, and anger.

Creating a new identity means leaving behind the version of the past that no longer serves us and building a completely different one. We cannot expect an enjoyable life if we resort to the same thoughts and attitudes with which we once survived our history. This identity must be a new way of being in life.

I also believe that in order to create a new identity, we must be brave and leave behind our past identity. It is filled with limiting aspects of our personality that we need to liberate. This includes silent agreements in which we promised the world we would not be our best selves; we wouldn't dazzle it with our light; we wouldn't unsettle it with our passion for living; we would travel little; we wouldn't pursue pleasure; we would be discreet, serious, boring, uneducated, and without aspirations; and we would do everything possible to go unnoticed.

The guy from whom I broke off my engagement had a recurring dream in which a dazzling light appeared in the darkness that caused him discomfort and great unease. "It was something I couldn't stand. It was you, Gina," he told me.

I have heard several people judge others who have turned their lives around. They criticize their achievements and successes, saying they are the result of luck or privileged conditions. Other people's happiness generates discomfort. It's an invitation to a party not everyone wants or can attend.

Creating a new identity is a solitary and sublime path, a secret freedom that no one can take from you. It's a breeze that is felt in the air. We've all known someone who is genuinely happy with what they have. Creating a new identity means leaving places where you are not invited and being in those where our essence can blossom to its fullest expression.

In the words of David Whyte's poem "The Opening of Eyes": [26]

*That day I saw beneath dark clouds*
*the passing light over the water*
*and heard the voice of the world speaking out.*
*I knew then as I had before*
*Life is no passing memory of what has been,*
*nor the remaining pages of a great book waiting to be read.*
*It is the opening of eyes long closed.*
*It is the vision of far off things*
*seen for the silence they hold.*
*It is the heart after years*
*of secret conversing*
*speaking out loud in the clear air.*
*It is Moses in the desert*

---

[26] David Whyte is an Anglo-Irish poet who describes his work as being based on "the conversational nature of reality." His book *The Heart Aroused: Poetry and Preservation of the Soul in Corporate America*, is one of his most successful creations. David travels around the world with people interested in poetry and nature. I attended a course he taught in San Francisco, California, shortly after the COVID-19 pandemic.

*fallen to his knees before the lit bush.*
*It is the man throwing away his shoes*
*as if to enter heaven*
*and finding himself astonished,*
*opened at last,*
*fallen in love with solid ground.*

Dr. Joe Dispenza has conducted extensive research on this topic and uses meditation practices to heal diseases, some of them terminal, and to generate personality changes and create a new identity.

For five years, I attended his conferences and workshops. There, I had the opportunity to practice meditation and work with the power of manifestation (by visualizing objects or situations during the meditation space and creating or seeing them materialize in the physical world). Many of these meditations are guided, meaning that instructions are given to direct concentration and breathing.

Almost all of the meditations are focused on creating a new identity. A new being awaits us in the future that has already occurred in the psychic dimension ready for us to bring it into form in our present, this physical and earthly world.

This is a powerful and interesting idea, as it invites us to reflect on the fact that "somewhere" outside time and space, there is a "complete and more authentic self" that is available to us, a possibility, and an opportunity we should not miss. In this dimension where everything is possible, and we are not divided by the materiality of our body, there is health, harmony, and unity in everything we are.

Once, on my way to a conference, I met a woman at the airport. She was paralyzed and in a wheelchair as a result of having fallen from the seventh-floor balcony of a building and had been unable to walk for 15 years. Doctors told her she would never walk again due to severe spinal injuries. She, too, was attending Dr. Joe's course.

I talked with her over the seven days of our meditation training, and she told me she felt something changing inside her body. One day before the training ended, during one of the guided meditations, she suddenly stood up from her chair. "I can feel my legs," she told me.

It was amazing to see that. When I asked her how it had happened, she said that in the meditation, she saw herself very clearly standing and supported by her legs: "I didn't imagine it; it was real," she added.

She was able to connect to that dimension where only health exists and managed to bring forth that information from the psychic plane to the material one. It's something that would seem unbelievable if someone else had told me about it. This is the reach that the journey inward can have. It's something we do every day without realizing it—we materialize what we think without paying attention to it, and without understanding that we are co-creators of our reality.

Being in this process involves taking a quantum leap within our existence, but it is important to note that thoughts alone do not work to materialize the reality we want; we need to feel it in our heart. Ideas don't have the strength to take shape; emotions serve as the fuel for it to happen.[27]

The HeartMath Institute in California, has been studying the heart for over 20 years. [28] Since 1991, it has promoted the conscious work that can be done by focusing on this organ, and provides practical tools that help connect us with the essence of who we really are. It has researched and developed the scientific basis that allows us to connect the mind with the heart and deepen the connection between people. This methodology reduces stress, increases resilience (the ability to adapt well to a traumatic event), and opens natural intuition to make better decisions.

---

[27] A quantum leap is an abrupt change, sudden increase, or dramatic advance. Quantum leap is rarely used in scientific contexts, but it originated as a synonym of quantum jump, which describes an abrupt transition (as of an electron, an atom, or a molecule) from one discrete energy state to another.

[28] The HeartMath Institute, based in Boulder Creek, California, is an institution dedicated to empowering individuals, families, groups, and organizations, to enhance their life experiences using tools that enable them to better recognize and access their intuitive insight and heart intelligence. Their stated mission is to co-create a kinder, more compassionate world by conducting interconnectivity research and providing heart-based, science-proven tools for raising humanity's baseline consciousness from separation and discord to compassionate care and cooperation. For more about them, please visit: www.HeartMath.org.

It has been discovered that the heart is not just an organ that pumps blood but also has its own "mind"; that is, it has neurons similar to those in the brain. For the ancient Egyptians (circa 3300 BC), the heart was the most important organ in the body, because it represented the physical place where the truth was located. It was left inside the body after mummification, and a mummy buried without it could not be reborn, thus having a final death. The heart can tell the truth about what we feel or what we think is true or not. For example, when we lie, it accelerates; the same happens if it feels love or hate.

The heart and brain are connected and work together in the expression of emotions. According to the HeartMath Institute, the electromagnetic field that the human heart projects outward can reach a distance of up to five meters. Information and energy are transmitted through this electromagnetic field, and it is how this organ contacts all systems of the body.

What I find surprising is that the heart receives information from our surroundings 4.5 seconds before the brain does, which means that this organ can anticipate what will happen before the brain registers the same.

A remarkably interesting study was conducted by placing electrodes on the chest of a group of people to record their heart's electrical activity. They had to watch a video that presented different situations of joy, pain, suffering, fear, love, and wonder. It was observed that 4.5 seconds before the images appeared, the heart already knew what was going to happen, and the electrical signals changed.

Below, I share some simple steps that can help you in your search for a new identity. They are listed in no particular order and can be used jointly or individually, depending on where you are in the process:

## How to Create a New Identity

- **Seek New Experiences** – Learn to play an instrument, paint, attend a literary workshop, take cooking classes, climb a mountain, or try an activity that interests you that you've never done before.
- **Visualize the Future** – Imagine what you want and notice the emotions that go with what you desire. You might want to keep a log in which you write a description of how that future feels. Ask yourself questions like: ***Who am I in that future? How do I feel about living that new reality? What have I discovered? How have my eyes opened?*** In this way, you align your emotions with your thoughts and feel the ideas. Or you can do the exercises presented in the Rewriting One's Own Story section in Part One.
- **Pay Attention to Your Heart** – A simple exercise I do in therapy is to ask patients to place their hands on their chest and ask their heart if what they think at that moment is true or not. A yes or no will appear in your mind almost instantly.
- **Reflect on What Your Name Means to You** – Our given name is a fundamental part of our personal identity, and it is known that it can determine a person's destiny. In Judaism, someone's name is changed after surviving an illness or accident. In Family Constellation therapy, it has been observed that people who have the same name as an ancestor have the same life issues or dilemmas to resolve.

In my youth, I attended a workshop with the Mexican writer and journalist Ángeles Mastretta.

The theme for the workshop was Reconciliation with the Name. My full name is Regina, like my paternal grandmother, and I decided to attend the workshop because I was interested in working on the discomfort and rejection I felt toward my name. In elementary school, I hated hearing my name when the attendance roll was called; I really felt embarrassed.

I discovered that the name Regina represented everything bad for me. My father used to shout it when he fought with me, reprimanded me, or made me feel that he didn't love me. He also called me Regina when he prohibited me from using my voice or I tried to set boundaries. And he called me Gina or "Mi Alma (my soul)" when he was pleased with me, when I was a "good daughter," or when I satisfied him.

Finally, I made peace with my name. *Regina* is a Latin word that means "powerful queen," and I think it represents the force of resilience within me. At the end of the workshop, Mastretta asked us to baptize ourselves with a name: I chose Mariposa (Butterfly).

The duality I have experienced with my name is still there; in doctors' appointments and pharmacy records, I always appear with different names; sometimes I am Regina, sometimes Gina, and the surnames sometimes are my maiden name and other times my married name. I have never given the same name anywhere. The only thing that has saved me from having a single name identity are official documents.

Finally, I was able to choose to become an author with the name under which I sign this book. Mariposa is my secret name, and I can now coexist with Regina.

All of this is involved in creating a new identity.

# 16

# TOUCHING THE SOUL THROUGH THE BODY

My teacher, Rabbi Kanner, says that the way to know our soul is through the body. I agree with him. Earthly experiences are designed to confront us. Our choices can be oriented toward acting instinctively or with awareness.

When I decided to participate in a course he teaches, he initially asked me, "What transformation are you seeking?"

"To bring God down into my heart, not just to believe in Him intellectually," I replied.

He ended the conversation by telling me, "That will happen, but first, you need to connect the soul with the body."

That was a great revelation as, for a long time, I believed that the spiritual dimension was separate from the physical world. Now I understand that our concrete actions are a spiritual expression. Beyond any religion, the way we care for our body, how we use it, how we dress, what we eat, and how we use our words, are a representation of our inner world. One way of being in life is to enjoy it through the body. It is the wrapper we take everywhere, our business card, the vehicle of consciousness. It is the bodily individuality that allows us to have "free will."

I remember an experience I had on a school trip. It was a project where a group of middle-schoolers spent half a year abroad. The first few days, I felt sad and missed Mexico.

One afternoon, I locked myself in the room for a couple of hours because I wanted to cry without having to explain. In front of me was a full-length mirror. I looked at my face for two hours and focused on my eyes. Suddenly, something beyond my body was there; my soul was escaping through the gaze. Literally. I could see it. And I had a conversation with it, one without words.

Many years later, as part of my professional therapy practice, I began including the exercise of looking at oneself in the mirror with intention. Patients have had mystical experiences they can't describe when they do this exercise. Loving what we are includes loving our body. Personally, I have had great challenges—enough to one day write a whole book about it.

The relationship we have with our body is so important that in religions and cultures there are various rituals to honor and connect it with the earth and with God. In Judaism, there is the Brith Milah (Hebrew for "the covenant of the word"), in which the newborn boy is circumcised to symbolize his covenant with God. In Christianity, there is baptism, a sacrament in which holy water is poured on the newborn's head or they are submerged in water as a symbol of purification. In the Christian mass, the host is placed in the mouth until it dissolves; it is a circular wafer as an offering or a bloodless sacrifice.

In short, there are many rituals that use the body as a symbolic vehicle of connection with the heavenly world.

Meditation is an important practice for being in life and achieving spiritual connection. Any type of meditative practice fulfills this purpose. It is also important to use intuition to listen to the body and create the optimal scenarios for it to express itself. We need to turn the instinctual into poetry and the body into inspiration.

Below you find some ways to listen to the body.

## Touching Your Soul through Your Body

- **Consider the Body** – The word "consider" comes from the Latin *considerare*, which means "to observe the stars carefully"; that is, "to be in harmony with the stars." As it relates to the body, it implies our determination to listen to our body in order to be in harmony with it. For example, the body has its own particular language through which it communicates its health status and gives us warnings about what we need to do to regulate it. If we feel sleepy, we should sleep; eat only when hungry; and give ourselves a hug if we need contact without waiting for someone else to do it. Miley Cyrus's 2023 song

"Flowers,"[29] which has become a sort of anthem, especially among the female audience, speaks precisely about this:

*I can buy myself flowers*
*write my name in the sand*
*talk to myself for hours . . .*
*I can take myself dancing*
*and I can hold my own hand . . .*
*Yeah, I can love me better than you can . . .*

- **Pamper the Body** – Pamper can be said to involve feeling the body through all the senses. Caress it; give it a new haircut; change its style of dress; take it for a walk; use its senses to admire landscapes, to listen to nature and music, to immerse it in water to free it from the weight of gravity, to dance freely. Currently, there are many rituals around the body to connect it with a spiritual dimension. For example, the cacao ceremony, sound bowls, and hugging trees, among others.
- **Nourish the Body** – "Nourish" is a synonym for feeding—not just sensorially but with emotions and artistic, playful, spiritual experiences, among others. As for food, Geneen Roth, in her book *When Food Is Love*, explains that a person's life is summed up on their plate; the way you eat, what you eat, and when and why you eat reflect your inner universe. Here, the emotional wound determines our relationship with food.

[29] "Flowers" ©2023. Lyrics by Miley Cyrus, Michael Pollack, and Gregory Aldae Hein.

17

# FORGIVING AN APOLOGY NOT RECEIVED

Of all the healing processes, forgiving an apology not received is the most challenging task we will face before releasing our wound.

In most cases, the authors who wrote our childhood story with a dagger never cleaned the blood spilled in their acts and words. In none of the clinical cases I shared, including my personal case, did we receive an apology.

After all these years of experience, I have concluded that this is how the educational program is designed. When the perpetrator does not acknowledge that they have hurt us, we must resort to our inner wisdom to save ourselves from exile.

And so, we become wanderers, sailors, explorers, magicians . . . The apology that never appears is an echo in our gut, it eats at our soul, and we patiently wait for someone to ask for our forgiveness.

But they never come. They were never there—neither the people who need to apologize nor the apologies and explanations themselves. It doesn't matter what their reasons are. It is as if the apology we are waiting for will allow us to take our place in this world, yet we remain there, in the desert, without answers or explanations, because those we hope will apologize to us do not believe we deserve them.

In reality, none of this matters. It's not about them; it's about us. It's our story. An unreceived apology is our one-way ticket, a passport to far-off lands, because from a distance, we regain perspective. We need to recover more than to forgive them.

Am I exaggerating? Does it seem harsh to hear? Absolutely not.

What I have just stated barely touches the devastation of suffering. I'm talking about the real damage—the damage that has ruined and destroyed the spirit, the damage that has set the forest of our being on fire, leaving the soul in ashes—that damage.

I don't know how to name it. Many will find it uncomfortable. Others will feel outraged. And there are those who will find it astonishing to choose not to forgive. The perpetrators of such damage are voracious, a plague that ravages the crop that could have been fertile, ensuring that their victims wither and die on the vine.

Forgiving an apology not received means immediately returning to the wound. There is no erasing and starting anew. We must travel as far as possible to a new land, make it our own, inhabit it, find a place without them.

Judaism celebrates the Day of Atonement, or Yom Kippur in Hebrew. The commemoration of this festival takes place in the Jewish month of Tishrei, which means "beginning." Yom Kippur marks the end of the "Days of Awe, or Days of Repentance," which start with the Jewish New Year, or Rosh Hashanah. For 10 days, it is believed that a person can influence God's plans for the coming year, since atonement offers an opportunity for people to change their fate through prayer, repentance, and direct forgiveness toward those they have hurt.

To perform the introspection of repentance, one fasts throughout the day to avoid any distractions; it is also a way to show the sacrifice of becoming aware of one's actions. The belief around this ritual is that one must reflect on how their relationship has been with others and see in what ways they have harmed them, because God cannot forgive what we have done to others. The repair must be directly toward the person we have hurt and then we can forgive ourselves for our actions.

Society pressurizes us to forgive our parents as a way of maintaining order and the comfort of silence. Admitting harm requires collective transformation: a search for awareness, taking responsibility, reparations toward victims, and creation of new values within the community. When we are forced to forgive we become a permanent victim. It is false forgiveness, because we genuinely feel outraged and cannot let go.

I shared this part of the book with some friends, curious to know what "forgiving an apology not received" sounds like in the voices of others. One friend was immediately angered when I read the first lines to him, saying: "Don't tell me I have to forgive, because if you do, I don't want to continue listening."

Some patients said that they realized how difficult it was for them to hear this ruthless truth, recognizing that they felt fear of "going against" everything they had been taught (they referred to "respecting and loving their parents no matter their actions"), precisely what Alice Miller exposes in *The Body Never Lies: The Lingering Effects of Hurtful Parenting*.

Regardless of perspective, this is a truth that requires hard emotional work in order to admit it. It would be impossible to try to share concrete steps to forgive an unreceived apology, since each person has a different path to follow. Even so, I will present a few:

- Under no circumstances should you force yourself to forgive someone who has not apologized to you.
- Do not wait for others' forgiveness to move forward in your life.
- Embark on a journey to new lands, far from everything that has hurt you; you don't have to stay in a place where you are not welcome.
- Work emotionally to validate your own wound. You do not need to justify your pain.
- Carry out the exercises suggested in Part Three for being in life with enjoyment.

In the words of poet David Whyte:[30]

> Forgiveness is a heartache and difficult to achieve because, strangely, it not only refuses to remove the original wound but actually brings us closer to its source. Getting closer to forgiveness is getting closer to the nature of the damage itself, being the only remedy, as we approach its raw center, we have to reimagine our relationship with it.

---

[30] David Whyte, *Consolations: The Solace, Nourishment and Underlying Meaning of Everyday Words* (Many Rivers Press, 2021).

# 18

# THE WOUND AS AN OPPORTUNITY

Together we have reached solid ground after a long process of understanding the origin of our emotional wound, its manifestations, its silences, and consequent tears. Recovering from a pain that has broken our existence is not easy. Some never achieve it.

We need to rest, caress the heart, and remember what we were before that moment when life ceased to belong to us. We need to gather the strength to rebuild ourselves, assemble the broken pieces, and glue them back together with our tears. We need to be our own source, and allow ourselves to drink long and often in order to quench the thirst our story left behind.

And when a crack opens through which we can understand what surviving has been about, we can begin anew. Geneen Roth expresses it like this: "Our problems are the passage that leads us to the wisdom of our healing."

In this book, I have shared the many different opportunities we have to work on our wound. It is always possible to start over as long as there is life. When we understand the origin of our suffering and manage to embrace it, the act of intrinsic acceptance frees us from the bond. It is in that moment of realization when we discover that we are not our wound that life shows who we really are.

At that moment, opportunities arise from the most unexpected places, because in abandonment, we discover our strength; in rejection, our self-love. Being able to find the opportunities amidst adversity is a sign that the wound has been left behind on the path.

The pilgrimage of healing is the most profound opportunity we can approach in life. To release the wound will guide us back to the true home we should have never left.

## Camino

### by David Whyte[31]

*The way forward, the way between things,*
*the way already walked before you,*
*the path disappearing and reappearing even*
*as the ground gave way beneath you,*
*the grief apparent only in the moment*
*of forgetting, then the river, the mountain,*
*the lifting song of the Sky Lark inviting*
*you over the rain-filled pass when your legs*
*had given up, and after,*
*it would be dusk and the half-lit villages*
*in evening light; other people's homes*
*glimpsed through lighted windows*
*and inside, other people's lives; your own home*
*you had left crowding your memory*
*as you looked to see a child playing*
*or a mother moving from one side of*
*a room to another, your eyes wet*
*with the keen cold wind of Navarre.*
*But your loss brought you here to walk*
*under one name and one name only,*
*and to find the guise under which all loss can live;*
*remember, you were given that name every day*
*along the way, remember, you were greeted as such,*
*and treated as such and you needed no other name,*
*other people seemed to know you even before*
*you gave up being a shadow on the road*
*and came into the light, even before you sat down,*
*broke bread and drank wine,*
*wiped the wind-tears from your eyes:*
*pilgrim they called you,*
*pilgrim they called you again and again. Pilgrim.*

---

[31] *Pilgrim*, by David Whyte (Many Rivers Press, 2012).

APPENDICES

# List of Exercises



# List of Clinical Cases

# Bibliography

**Aprende Institute**. "Para qué Sirven los Mantras y Cómo Crear el Tuyo."
https://aprende.com/blog/bienestar/meditacion/que-es-un-mantra/

**Cameron, Julia**. *The Artist's Way*. TarcherPerigee, 2016.

**Cyrulnik, Boris**. *Psicoecología. El entorno y las estaciones del alma.* Editorial Gedisa, 2021.

**De Unamuno, Miguel**. *The Private World: Selections from the Diario Intimo and Selected Letters 1890–1936 (Selected Works of Miguel de Unamuno, Vol. 2)*. Princeton University Press, 1985.

**Dispenza, Joe**. *Breaking the Habit of Being Yourself: How to Lose Your Mind and Create a New One*. Hay House Books, 2012.

**Duras, Marguerite**. *The War: A Memoir*. The New Press, 1994.

**Durkheim, Emile**. *Las formas elementales de la vida religiosa.* Colofón Ediciones, 1912/1991.

**Fisher, Robert**. *The Knight in Rusty Armor*. Wilshire Book Company, 1987.

**Frank, Anne**. *The Diary of Anne Frank*. Bantam Books, 1997.

**Freud, Sigmund**. *The Interpretation of Dreams: The Complete and Definitive Text*. Basic Books, 2010.

**Gogol, Nikolai**. *Diary of a Madman, The Government Inspector, and Selected Stories*. Penguin Classics, 2006.

**Han, Byung-Chul**. *The Disappearance of Rituals: A Topology of the Present.* Polity Press, 2020.

**Huezo, Tatiana**. *El Eco*. Chulada Films & Radiola Films, 2023.

**Jung, Carl Gustav**. *The Archetypes and The Collective Unconscious. Collected Works of C.G. Jung.* Princeton University Press, 1981.

———. *Memories, Dreams, Reflections.* Vintage Books, 1989.

———. *The Red Book.* W.W. Norton and Company, 2009.

**Kafka, Franz**. *Metamorphosis and Other Stories.* Penguin Classics, 2008.

———. *Diaries*. Schocken Books, 2024.

**Katie, Byron**. *Who Would You Be Without Your Story? Dialogues with Byron Katie.* Hay House Publishing, 2008.

**Katie, Byron** with **Stephen Mitchell**. *Loving What Is: Four Questions that Can Change Your Life*, Revised Edition. Harmony Books, 2021.

**Klugman, Rabbi Eliyahu Meir**. *Rabbi Samson Raphael Hirsch. Architect of Judaism for the Modern World.* Artscroll Mesorah, 1996.

**Krauze, Ethel**. *Desnudando a la musa: ¿qué hay detrás del talento literario?* Conaculta, 2012.

**Manheimer, Eric**. *Twelve Patients: Life and Death at Bellevue Hospital* (The Inspiration for the NBC Drama New Amsterdam). Grand Central Publishing, 2013.

**Maturana, Humberto** & **J. Francisco Varela**. *The Tree of Knowledge: The Biological Roots of Human Understanding.* Shambhala Publications, 1992.

**Mead, G.R.S**. *The Chaldean Oracles. Echoes From the Gnosis, volume VIII.* CreateSpace Independent Publishing Platform, 2015.

**Miller, Alice**. *The Body Never Lies: The Lingering Effects of Hurtful Parenting.* W.W. Norton & Company, 2006.

———. *The Drama of the Gifted Child and the Search for the True Self.* Basic Books, 2008.

**Palazzoli, Mara Selvini**. *Self-Starvation: From the Intrapsychic to the Transpersonal Approach to Anorexia Nervosa.* Human Context Books, 1974.

**Pliny, The Elder**. *Natural History. A Selection.* Penguin Classics, 1991.

**Porto, J. Perez** & **M. Merino**. "Definition of Mantra: What It Is, Significance and Concept, and Definition" ("*Definición de mantra: Qué es, Significado y Concepto, Definicion.*"), 27 October 2010, last modified September 27, 2022, https://definicion.de/mantra/

**Progoff, Ira**. *At a Journal Workshop: Writing to Access the Power of the Unconscious and Evoke Creative Ability.* Penguin Publishing Group, 1992.

———. *At a Journal Workshop.* Dialogue House Library, 1975.

———. *Process Meditation.* Dialogue House Library, 1980.

**Quintas, Cipri**. *Sawubona: El secreto del verdadero éxito.* Alienta Editorial, Barcelona, Spain, 2022.

**Rappaport, Roy**. *Pigs for the Ancestors: Ritual in the Ecology of a New Guinea People.* Waveland Press Inc., 2000.

**Saint-Exupéry, Antoine**. *The Wisdom of the Sands.* University of Chicago Press, 1984.

**Schulner, David**. *New Amsterdam*. Pico Creek Productions, 2018.

**Selvini Palazzoli, Mara**. *Self-Starvation: From the Intrapsychic to the Transpersonal Approach to Anorexia Nervosa*. Human Context Books, 1974.

**Shinoda Bolen, Jean**. *Goddesses in Everywoman: Powerful Archetypes in Women's Lives*. Harper Paperbacks. New York, N.Y., 2014.

**Shlezinger, Rabbi Aharon David**. *Pirkei Avot Explicado: Con los comentarios de Rashi y Rabí Ovadia de Bartenura* (Spanish Edition). Independently published, 2021.

**Snunit, Michal**. *The Soul Bird*. Hyperion, 1999.

**Sontag, Susan**. *As Consciousness Is Harnessed to Flesh: Journals and Notebooks*, 1964–1980. Picador, 2013.

**Terman, L. M**. *The Measurement of Intelligence: An Explanation of and a Complete Guide for the Use of the Stanford Revision and Extension of the Binet-Simon Intelligence Scale*. Houghton Mifflin Co., 1916.

———. *The Stanford Revision and Extension of the Binet-Simon Scale for Measuring Intelligence*. Warwick & York, Inc., 1917.

———. *Genetic Studies of Genius*. Stanford University Press, 1925.

———. "Autobiography of Lewis Terman". In Carl A. Murchison, and Edwin G. Boring. *A History of Psychology in Autobiography*. Clark University Press, 1930.

**Terman, L. M.**, and **Merrill, M. A**. *Measuring Intelligence: A Guide to the Administration of the New Revised Stanford-Binet Tests of Intelligence*. Houghton Mifflin Company, 1937.

**Terman, L. M., Oden. M. H.**, and **Bayley, N**. *The Gifted Child Grows Up: Twenty-five Years' Follow-Up of a Superior Group (Genetic Studies of Genius, Vol. 4)*. Stanford University Press, 1947.

**Turner, Victor**. *The Forest of Symbols: Aspects of Ndembu Ritual.* Cornell University Press, 1970.

———.“Social Dramas and Stories about Them” in *Critical Inquiry, Vol. 7, no. 1*. University of Chicago Press, 1980.

**Vaillant, George E**. *Adaptation to Life*. Harvard University Press, 1998.

———. *Aging Well: Surprising Guideposts to a Happier Life*. Little, Brown & Co., 2002.

**Whyte, David**. *The Heart Aroused: Poetry and Preservation of the Soul in Corporate America.* Crown Currency, 1996.

———. *Pilgrim*. Many Rivers Press, 2012.

———. *Consolations: The Solace, Nourishment and Underlying Meaning of Everyday Words*. Many Rivers Press, 2021.

# Acknowledgments

The writing of a book comes to a close when all the parties involved in its creation converge at the same point: its birth. What better time to thank all those who accompanied me along the journey!

I thank my family—my husband Aaron for his patience and collaboration in covering for my absence while I was at the keyboard, sometimes for weeks without rest; and my children Marcos and Alexa, for the enthusiasm and sparkle with which they supported my creative process, as well as their empathy, and for motivating me to fulfill this dream.

To my sister Jacky—for her joy and love, which propelled me in moments of doubt and for her complicity, support, and strength in helping me navigate the darkest nights of the soul. Thank you for always believing in me.

To my nephews Batia and Salo, for the kindness of their eyes, the beauty of their souls, and the vital energy they always inject in every encounter.

To my friend, teacher, workshop leader, and advisor Ethel Krauze—for giving me the confidence to release my words to the world, for accompanying me every step of the way with generosity, respect, and commitment, for helping me in my education as a writer, and above all, for giving me her humanity. I am fortunate.

To my dear friends and colleagues Ana Laura Rojo and Roberto Musi—for their unconditional friendship and the enjoyment with which we have shared life, for their generous work providing the blurbs for the back cover and, above all, for being confidants and witnesses to my wound.

A book is the result of more than just the work of the author. I am deeply grateful to Inner Traditions and Findhorn Press for believing in this book—to Mahar Sperling and Sabine Weeke at Findhorn for their generous opportunity and their trust and belief in this project, and for their brave decision to take it around the world. Thanks

Sabine, for your warmth, companionship, commitment, and joy. I also want to thank my editor, Nicky Leach, for her impeccable and professional work, keen eye for details, and wonderful suggestions. Thanks for your sincere and precise support, which has ensured that we have a valuable book in our hands. It is such a joy to work with as dedicated a professional as you!

To my dear agents Paulina Vieitez and Gerardo Cardenas who, with their tireless spirit, ensured my book reached a wonderful port beyond the shores of Mexico. Thank you for your warmth, professionalism, and unique ability to see the good in all things. I am honored to belong to the PaGe family. Additional thanks to Gerardo, who is not only my agent and my friend, but also my translator. Thank you for sending these words into a great adventure, and for your passion to ensure that people in other parts of the world will read it.

The journey of this book began in Spanish, and I want to thank Larisa Curiel and Paloma González at Urano who opened the door to this proposal first, for their dedication, hard work, and collaboration to accompany me in this first part of the process.

To my teacher, Fernando Díaz San Miguel—for reading and reviewing my text. His observations and questions allowed me to reconsider some concepts.

To my chosen family: Maribel Bonilla, Sara Cabrera, Jackie Wasserteil, Karen Trajtman, Karen Coppock, Susy Memun, Luz Elena Solís, Lis Claverie, Anita Achar, Annie Heitler, and Dalia Punsky—for being witnesses and life companions.

To my patients, who for almost three decades have humbly given me their stories—for trusting me, and above all, for helping me become who I am today.

To my wound—for filling my life with opportunities.

And to you—for it is you who will bring this book to life through your reading.

# Index

# About the Author

**Gina Goldfeder (Regina Razón Goldfeder), Ph.D.,** is a therapist and writer. With a B.A. in Clinical Psychology from Universidad Anáhuac, Mexico City, and a Master's and Ph.D. in Individual and Couples' Therapy from the Mexican Institute for Couples, Gina also holds a Master's in Creative Writing and a Literature Diploma.

Since 1995, Gina has led a therapy practice for individuals and couples in Mexico City, and she has taught courses in psychology at the Universidad Iberoamericana.

Her own skills have been enhanced from trainings with noted specialists, such as Dr. Joe Dispenza, Geneen Roth, Brené Brown, Byron Katie, and Jon Progoff, and specific courses on Progoff's Intensive Journaling, Julia Cameron's *The Artist's Way*, the HeartMath system as taught at the HeartMath Institute, dream interpretation, Theta healing, and psychodrama.

Since 2019, Gina has been a frequent guest on Mexico's *Arriba con Mayte* radio show, talking about issues of human development. Gina meditates daily and is passionate about reading, writing, and traveling.

For more information, email her at **ginarazon@hotmail.com** or contact her through Facebook or Instagram (**dra._gina_goldfeder**).

FINDHORN PRESS

*Life-Changing Books*

Learn more about us and our books at
www.findhornpress.com

For information on the Findhorn Foundation:
www.findhorn.org